DEDICATION

TO SYLVIA KELLY
REMEMBERED BY SO MANY
FOR HER ENTHUSIASM AND EFFORTS
FOR HENLEAZE

HENLEAZE CONNECTIONS:

SOME FASCINATING FOLK AND FACTS

Veronica Bowerman

TABLE OF CONTENTS

ACKNOWLEDGEMENTS

Many thanks to the following people who have enabled me to complete this publication:

VERNON TOTTLE and MARION SCHIESSER (née TOTTLE) are former local residents as well as volunteer proofreaders and editors. They both made contact by email in 2014 following the publication of HENLEAZE JUNIOR SCHOOL: THE EARLY YEARS.

Since the publication of the second edition of The Henleaze Book in 2006 many other people have been in touch with local and social history information about Henleaze. Some really historic photos also have also been submitted – often from family albums – for readers to share and enjoy.

Many thanks to the many contributors who have helped create this new book on Henleaze. They have been acknowledged in the respective articles.

WIKIPEDIA were able to provide some additional relevant and often fascinating information about some of the events. Do use and support this free encyclopaedia. /http://en.wikipedia.org/wiki/Main_Page/

PREFACE

This publication, Henleaze Connections, highlights some of the diverse and interesting folk who have lived in Henleaze from the 1800s. The Romans passed through the area much earlier but we can find no conclusive evidence that they stayed for any length of time.

The book also mentions a few people who have left their mark on Henleaze although they did not reside there. Some others only lived in Henleaze for a few short years but then went on to make their impact elsewhere, some globally.

The range of different occupations is astonishing. These are some that have been mentioned:

Actor, best-selling author, builder, Caribbean schoolgirl, chocolate entrepreneur , corsetiere, cricketer, dredging fleet owner, Egyptologist, footballer, headmistress, humanist, journalist, miller, missionary, physicist, timber merchant, WWII hero etc. etc.

The latter part of the book covers various properties in the area and their occupants as well some updates on some of the interesting historic buildings and lodges. Many people will remember shopping in Harbury Road. It is interesting to read about the changes that have taken place there over the years.

One former resident revealed details of his old prep school which survived six moves and remained in existence for 76 years.

Many of the 80 plus fascinating photos have come from private collections and have never been published before.

The reader may find that a few of the people included are already known to him/her. Some may seem to be quite ordinary, but all of them have played their part in the enthralling social history of the Henleaze area. Enjoy!

PART 1

MORE ABOUT THE ROMANS IN HENLEAZE

KELLAWAY AVENUE FIND

The Henleaze Book highlighted the find of a small figurine of the god Mercury unearthed in Golden Hill in 1935 by Mr Bryant. It is thought to be approximately 2,200 years old. The figurine which is made of copper alloy, is approximately five centimetres high and is now located in the Bristol Museum.

SPRINGFIELD GROVE FIND

In October 2012, Julian Lea-Jones, local historian, dug up a coin in the garden of his former home in Springfield Grove. Careful washing revealed a standing figure holding what appeared to be a staff and globe, with one foot raised on something - see photo of the reverse side of the coin; the other side had a diademed head.

A numismatist identified it for Julian as a coin of the Emperor Valentinian II, AD383 – 392, (similar ones have been found at Kings Weston). How did one of his coins, minted anywhere from Constantinople to Alexandria, end up in Henleaze?

For more information about Julian's work see http://history4u.info/

MOSAIC FLOOR MYSTERY

Jilly John, daughter of Ruby Lismore (née Langdon), who attended St Margaret's School, Henleaze Park in the 1920s and 1930s, says that her mother remembers clearly the existence of a mosaic floor out in the grounds of the school, quite large and well-preserved -though not cared-for. The girls were taken out to see it. They were always told it would probably have been the floor of a Roman villa. Jilly's mother can't unfortunately remember what the patterns were.

This is an excerpt of the 1881 OS map, when St Margaret's was a private residence known as Henleaze Park. No sign can be seen of the mosaic here?

Henleaze Farm is now known as the Briars at 7 Kenton Mews. Further details are given about this property later in the book.

If anyone has any further information on Roman findings in Henleaze please email henleazeheritage@gmail.com

PART 2

SOME FORMER HENLEAZE RESIDENTS

(1864 - 1892) AMELIA EDWARDS - BEST-SELLING AUTHOR, JOURNALIST & EGYPTOLOGIST

From 1864 until 1892 Amelia lived in the Larches, Eastfield, with Ellen Braysher who had been a friend of her mother's. Amelia's parents had died in 1860 within days of each other. Ellen and her husband John invited Amelia to stay with them in Kensington after this tragedy. Sadly, John died in 1863 so the decision was taken for Ellen and Amelia to move to Bristol. John and Ellen's daughter, Sarah, was living in Bath at that time and was roughly the same age as Amelia. Sarah died in 1864 aged 32, the year of the move, and was buried in Henbury. It appears from the various censuses that Ellen Braysher was the owner of the Larches and that Amelia was a boarder.

Amelia loved to travel. The income that she had accumulated in the 1850s from her employment as a journalist and the numerous short stories and books that she had published, enabled her now to do so. Countries she visited included Germany, Bavaria, Tyrol and Italy where she recorded her trips in great detail.

Amelia Edwards was one of a select band of authors invited by Dickens to contribute ghost stories to the Christmas numbers of his magazine All the Year Around. She is acknowledged as one of the best Victorian ghost story writers.

Amelia's second trip to Italy in 1872 was with a new travelling companion, Lucy Renshaw. They embarked on a standard tour of Italy visiting the sites of Rome, Venice and Naples where she witnessed the eruption of Mount Vesuvius. Lucy was an active companion and they decided to travel north to the Dolomites, and to undertake a difficult but ultimately rewarding mountain trek which resulted in Amelia's book "Untrodden Peaks and Unfrequented Valleys: a midsummer ramble in the Dolomites", the first of her travel books.

Her trip to Egypt - up the Nile from Cairo to Abu Simbel - took place in 1873. Her journey highlighted the ever-increasing threat from tourism and modern development to the irreplaceable ancient monuments. Furthermore, she was inspired to carry out research on hieroglyphics and complete a best seller in 1876 'A Thousand Miles up the Nile', which still remains in print. It makes fascinating reading, even today.

In 1877 Amelia said 'The work of destruction, meanwhile, goes on apace. There is no one to prevent it; there is no one to discourage it'. Then in 1879 a letter from Swiss Archaeologist Eduard Neville in the Morning Post outlined the need for foreign financial support for archaeology in Egypt as the country was teetering on the edge of bankruptcy. Amelia, with Reginald Stuart Poole of the Department of Coins and Medals of the British Museum, founded the Egypt Exploration Fund in 1882 in order, as announced at the time in several daily newspapers, 'to raise a fund for the purpose of conducting excavations in the Delta, which up to this time has been very rarely visited by travellers'.

Ultimately, Amelia's position as joint secretary of the Egypt Exploration Fund, her travels and her increasing number of publications provided the answer to Amelia's quest for meaningful work. Along with her new travelling companion, Kate Bradbury, she launched herself into a wildly ambitious speaking tour of America in 1889. As an Egyptologist, she was hailed as "the most learned woman in the world" by the New England Women's Press Association, which gave her a grand reception during her American tour in 1889–90.

Amelia's health had never been strong. In 1891 she succumbed to complications from exhaustion. She underwent surgery for breast cancer. She later developed a chest infection and went to a nursing home in Weston-super-Mare to help her recovery. Sadly she died there on 15 April 1892.

Ellen Braysher, the owner of Amelia's home, had died in January 1892, the same year. She had left her estate, including the Larches, to Amelia. In Amelia's will, her collection of Egyptian antiquities and also her library of books were bequeathed to University College London, where they formed the basis of the University's Egyptology Department. Amelia also endowed its chair in Egyptology, the first in the UK. Amelia's friend Kate Bradbury, who had accompanied her to the USA, was left to ensure that her wishes were carried out to benefit UCL (University College London) and the EEF (Egypt Exploration Fund). Kate later married the Professor of Egyptology at Oxford, Francis Llewellyn Griffith.

Amelia's grave, in Henbury (a suburb of Bristol) churchyard, is marked by an ankh. The ankh, also known as breath of life, the key of the Nile or crux ansata (Latin meaning "cross with a handle"), was the ancient Egyptian hieroglyphic character that read "life", a trilateral sign for the consonants Ayin-Nun-Het. See Wikipedia for more details: https://en.wikipedia.org/wiki/Ankh

Flinders Petrie (1853-1942) and Howard Carter (1874-1939) are among other Egyptologists to have received London blue plaques in recognition of their achievements and their association with buildings in the capital. Both benefited from the legacy of Amelia Edwards. On New

Year's Day, 1982 Mrs Doreen Layzell, local historian and writer conceived the idea that a commemorative plaque be erected to Amelia Edwards at the location of her Bristol home, the Larches in Eastfield, to celebrate the centenary of the founding of EEF (now known as the Egypt Exploration Society).

The Larches had been bombed in 1941 during WWII and, during the 1950s, two new houses were built on the site. In July 1982, from funds already collected by Doreen Layzell, the Memorial fund was officially founded to pay for the costs of the plaque. Doreen obtained permission beforehand from Dr and Mrs Maksimczyk, 22 Eastfield, to position the plaque on their boundary wall (the former wall of the Larches). The plaque was unveiled on 10 December 1982 by Miss Margaret Drower, MBE, FSA the Chairman of the Egypt Exploration Society. Nicholas Thomas, Director of the Bristol City Museum also attended the ceremony with other guests and spectators.

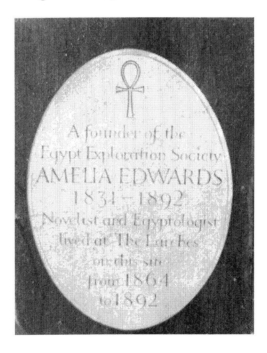

Amelia Edwards' (1831 - 1892) former London home - 19 Wharton Street, Clerkenwell, Islington - was honoured with an English Heritage Blue Plaque in 2015. Amelia lived there, with her family, when she first started her work as a writer before settling in Bristol, where she lived from 1864 - 1892.

In 2015 Dr Christopher Naunton, Director of the Egypt Exploration Society, said; 'Amelia Edwards' legacy to Egyptology is enormous. The Egypt Exploration Fund is today one of the leading institutions for archaeological research in Egypt, and its legacy and continued public funding is testimony to the widespread passion for the country's heritage which she generated through her writing, lecturing and influential contacts. Egyptology owes her an enormous debt.' In September, 2016 Churchill Retirement Living invited local residents to Amelia Lodge, Henleaze Terrace to see Dr Aidan Dodson, Chairman of the Egypt Exploration Society unveil the statue of Amelia Edwards that had been created by Emma Jean Kemp.

(1898 - 1912) CALEB BRUCE COLE - CHOCOLATE ENTREPRENEUR

Caleb Bruce Cole (1862 – 1912) bought Claremont House at an auction in 1898 for £9000 – well over the estimate of £6000 – £7000. The owner at that time, Mrs Julia Miller, had recently been widowed. Building had started on the house and other buildings in 1851 and was completed in 1853.

Set in 11 acres containing glasshouses and a conservatory, it then became the home of Caleb Bruce Cole and his family from 1898 to 1948. The borders reached Kellaway Avenue, Park Grove and Springfield Grove. The gardens were large and extended to the present Henleaze Park and Park Grove junction.

Sale particulars show that it was a substantial house, with dining room, drawing room, morning room (complete with telephone to stables), downstairs toilets with hot and cold water, kitchens, larders etc. There were cellars to accommodate beer and wine. Upstairs were seven bedrooms and two dressing rooms, and a bathroom with hot and cold water.

'The stabling and Gardener's cottage have recently been erected and are in perfect order. Badminton hounds also hunt the district.'

There was a partly-covered paved yard, and a second coach house with scullery and WC adjoining and two rooms over for the coachman. The cottage adjoins the stable and contains a sitting room, kitchen, larder, three bedrooms and offices and has a separate garden.

The sale particulars also stressed that the property had benefited from a large expenditure on drainage 'which is believed to be perfect.'

Caleb had bought out H J Packers & Co, the chocolate

manufacturers, in 1886 for £950 with a loan from his father. It took five years for the business to make a profit, and after 15 years, in 1901, the company had grown to such an extent that a new factory was commissioned at Greenbank in the Easton area of Bristol. The factory was built to the most modern standards of the day and included one of the very first sprinkler systems installed in a confectionery plant in Europe. The construction of the three factory blocks was planned largely by Caleb Bruce Cole's brother Horace who had joined the firm in 1900; the first steam engine there was fired up in November 1901.

The business grew steadily and between 1903 and 1912 sales increased by 250 per cent. More investment capital was raised in 1908 when the firm became a limited company.

Caleb Bruce Cole added a south wing to Claremont in 1909. Unfortunately in 1912 he died at the age of 50, but his wife Edith continued with the building work and in 1913 she doubled the size of the garage (next to Claremont Lodge) so that it would accommodate two motor cars and have an inspection pit with a tin for collecting oil. Edith Bruce Cole continued to live in

Claremont with her children until 1948 when it was sold to the council for £14,000. Henleaze Infant and Junior schools were then built in its grounds.

C. BRUCE COLE

"He was a man. Take him for all in all,
We shall not look upon his like again."

Caleb used to hire a train to take his family and animals on holiday to Evancoed in Wales and always made sure they had a banner on the side depicting Packer's Chocolates!

Throughout the time Caleb Bruce Cole was connected with the company he was universally admired and loved by the workforce as he was a man of his word, and had his employees' welfare as one of his chief considerations.

The last chocolate makers at Greenbank were Elizabeth Shaw in 2006. The portrait of Caleb is from their collection.

No part of the Claremont House appears to have been requisitioned during World War II. Henleaze Infant School was built on the former tennis courts of Claremont House and operated from there initially until its new purpose built school was completed in the early 1950s. Claremont itself has also operated as a School from this time and is now classified as a Community Special School.

Henleaze Infant School was initially known as Claremont Infants School. Derek Wilding attended the school at this time and has sent in his copy of the Claremont Henleaze Infants School Sports Day programme for 22 July 1950.

Bernard/Bunny Downs has detailed the following on Facebook:

"I started school at Claremont House before the Henleaze Infant School was built.
I actually saw both the infant and the junior schools being built. I think that would have been about 1950.The head of the infants was Mrs Tranfield and Mr Charles was head of the juniors."

Many thanks also to Margaret Short, a Henleaze Book reader, for supplying some of the additional information relating to the Bruce Cole family.

(1898 - 1967) MARGARET/MARGERY HARRISON - AUTHOR

The 1911 census shows the Harrison family living at 32 Downs Park East. Alfred William Harrison, the father, was head of a successful rope and sack making business in Bristol. One of his daughters, Margery (1898 - 1982) never married and, for a while, entered a nunnery. (She was a devout Catholic all her life).

Although she was known to her family as Marjie, she appeared on the 1911 census as Margery and later wrote under the name of Margaret. She lived at 19 Henleaze Gardens on the rather attic-like second floor until 1967 when she moved to a small house down in Westbury-on-Trym, after the death of her sister Olive.

Thanks to assistance from the Central Library's Reference Department, Bristol we have now ascertained that Margery wrote 15 romantic novels which were published between 1946 and 1961 under the name of Margaret Harrison. Three of these titles are available for study in the Reference Library:

Season of Song, A Time of Love and The Impatient Heart.

Perhaps she could be considered to have been the Barbara Cartland of Henleaze?

This is the complete list of her 15 novels obtained from the British Library: http://explore.bl.uk/

1 - Tomorrow's Daylight: London: John Gifford, 1946.

2 - The Season of Song: Martini Publications: London, 1949 [1950]. 1949.

3 - My ABC, devised and illustrated by Valerie Hodge, story told by M Harrison: Collins: London & Glasgow, [1950.] 1950.

4 - **A Time of Love:** London: Herbert Jenkins, 1952 [1953]. 1952.

5 - **The Impatient Heart:** London: Herbert Jenkins, 1953.

6 - **You'll love me yet:** London: Herbert Jenkins, 1954.

7 - **Trust thou thy Love:** London: Herbert Jenkins, 1955.

8 - **Where I Marry:** London: Herbert Jenkins, 1955.

9 - **A Joy more Gentle: London: Herbert Jenkins, 1956.**

10 - **The Sweetness of Forgiving:** London: Herbert Jenkins, 1956.

11 - **Love like a Shadow:** London: Herbert Jenkins, 1957.

12 - **The Starless Night:** London: W. H. Allen, 1958.

13 - **Legacy of Love: London: W. H. Allen, 1959.**

14 - **The Love of Leila:** London: W. H. Allen, 1960.

15 - **Beyond all telling: London: W. H. Allen, 1961.**

Margery died in 1982.

(1911 - 1933) STANLEY HUGH BADOCK - INDUSTRIALIST & HENLEAZE LAND MANAGER/OWNER

Stanley Hugh Badock (1867 – 1945) appears on 1871 census aged 3 residing at Badminton House, Westbury-on-Trym with his father, William F Badock, a mahogany merchant, his mother Miriam, a school mistress, and his three siblings Miriam – 14, Edith – 7, and Percy – 5.

Stanley joined Capper Pass, a smelting and refining company, straight from Clifton College around 1885. His sister Edith was by then the wife of Alfred Pass's nephew Henry C Trapnell, the company's solicitor. The 1891 census shows Stanley as a smelter, the 1901 one as head smelter and the 1911 as leadsmith director. Alfred Pass died in October, 1905 but remained as sole director until the middle of that year when Stanley Badock presided over the AGM on his behalf. Under the terms of Alfred's will, Stanley was appointed first president of the Capper Pass Board. In 1905 Stanley had bought the Holmwood estate and lived in the house with his wife Edith and their family. The history of Holmwood House and the estate located at the top of Channells Hill can be traced back to the early 1700s. Apart from the house with its stables, outbuildings and gardens etc, Stanley also bought the field east of the house, the majority of the wood later named after him and a pond in the wood (complete with weir). His ambitious ornamental landscaping and planting scheme extended along the Trym valley, linking Holmwood gardens with those at Southmead Manor House.

From 1908 – 1909 Stanley was Sheriff of Bristol and from 1911 became lessee of Henleaze Lake. In 1924 Stanley Badock bought 83 acres belonging to the Llewellin family, which included Henleaze Lake. He gave the Swimming Club a five year lease then and later sold it on to them in 1933.

In April 1937, his gift of the wood on his estate to Bristol Corporation was for perpetuity, but this was conditional on them also giving over 15 acres of their adjacent land for the same purpose. Following these transactions, the name 'Badock's Wood' came into existence. Under the Deed of Gift, Bristol Corporation was to maintain an un-climbable iron fence along the western boundary of the land. Also, no structures could be erected except such buildings and works 'as was necessary to protect the lands.' See Friends of Badock's Wood http://www.fobw.org.uk/

Badock Hall, one of the halls of residence of the University of Bristol, opened in 1964. It was named after Sir Stanley Hugh Badock, a benefactor and former Pro-Chancellor, Treasurer and Chairman of the University Council. In 1943 he had received an Honorary Doctorate of Law and was also knighted.

Sir Stanley Badock died in December 1945 and the National Children's Home subsequently purchased Holmwood.

(1920 - 1927) ERIC MCNEILL - MINISTER

In 2014 Jane Sleigh made contact by email regarding her grandfather Frederic Ernest McNeill, minister from 1920- 1927 of the then Congregational Church in Waterford Road, Henleaze. 'My grandfather lived in Dublin Crescent before he moved into Rouncot (the thatched cottage on Henleaze Road which was one of two lodges for Henleaze Park House). Allegedly, my grandmother Marie Eileen Lucy who was always known as Eileen (née Philp) lived next door/ nearby. Prior to this she lived in a flat overlooking the Downs, in Redland Road. She attended Colston Girls' School. One of her jobs was a piano teacher, I believe. She was the youngest of four, having three brothers.'

Eric McNeill, as he was known at that time, was ordained at Henleaze

Congregational Church on Monday, 11 October, 1920 as can be seen from the notice. He had entered Hackney Theological College after the First World War and was ordained after four years. His first church was Henleaze, where he was also married in 1925.

The manse at that time was a rented property known as Rouncot, the thatched cottage on Henleaze Road. Eric (b.1894) had two sisters Jessie (b.1896) and Julie (b.1900). They are pictured here at the gate on a visit.

'My grandparents were members of the church tennis club. It was called the Grasshoppers.

'Eric Mc Neill is shown smoking a pipe third from the right on the back row of the Tennis Club affiliated to the Church. Eric and his wife Eileen also used to go swimming in nearby Henleaze Lake.'

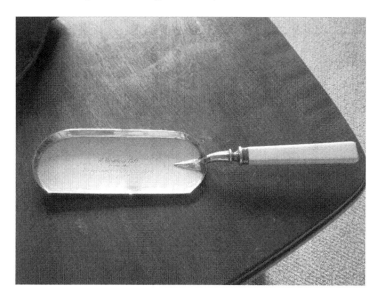

Eric and Eileen were married at the church on 4 July 1925. The Grasshoppers Tennis Club gave them a silver crumb tray which their son Roderic now has.

It is thought that the members of the Grasshoppers Tennis Club may have played at several different locations – perhaps initially on the courts in the grounds of Henley Park Mansions and maybe later at Tennessee Grove from 1926 where it may then have been renamed Henleaze Lawn Tennis Club. At that time the mansion was being converted into apartments. Edward Corner, Church Secretary in the 1920s, had been responsible for the provision of two grass courts and a wooden pavilion, possibly the one pictured here, for the use of church members. It appears that a tennis club was set up just after the First

World War by URC/Henleaze Congregational Church members and used almost exclusively by the Church's Young Peoples Fellowship (YPF), the youth club – this could have been the Grasshoppers Tennis Club?

This photo shows Eric and Eileen Mc Neill at Rouncot, the manse, after their wedding on 4 July, 1925. The best man on the left was Stuart Hibberd and the Matron of Honour was Gracie Pope. Eileen's brother on the right, Leslie Philp, gave her away.

Eric, who was interested in amateur dramatics, can be clearly seen in the back row second from the left. This photo appears to have been taken at one of the shows at the Church in the 1920s – details of the production are unknown to date.

The photo showing the car and surrounding crowd after the wedding on 4 July, 1925 was taken on Henleaze Road looking up towards the main shopping area and Northumbria Drive. The wall on the other side of Henleaze Road was removed some years later and the land there subsequently occupied by a garage. The Drive now lies behind the hoarding and the building with the white roof.

1920s photo of the exterior of the Church looking across Waterford Road, near the Henleaze Road junction. The interior photo also dates from 1920s. In 1927 Eric took the ministry at Henley-on-Thames where their children, Judith and Roderic, were born.

Photos, including the ones of the Church, are courtesy of the McNeill/Sleigh family.

(1920s/1930s) JOAN SANDERSON - SCHOOLGIRL & ACTRESS

Joan (1912 – 1992) was born in Bristol and attended Northumberland House School for Girls. She started acting at school where she appeared in 'The Rivals' in 1934. Joan is dressed as a footman third from the left on the photo.

She spent several seasons at Stratford-upon-Avon where her roles included Goneril in King Lear, Constance in King John, and Queen Margaret in Richard III. Her final stage career performance, 1981, was in the production of "Anyone for Denis" at the Whitehall Theatre in London's West End.

Her notable television performances included Miss Doris Ewell in Please Sir (1969) and an episode of Fawtly Towers (1975) as the selectively deaf Mrs Richards.

(1920s - 1960s) EMILY CASWILL - CORSETIERE

Sue Smith, nee Wollen-Bidgood, made contact with the Henleaze Book and provided two historical photos of Emily Caswill. We were subsequently able to give Sue details of local resident Liz Cameron who was able to supply some great additional details, hence this updated version!

Emily Jane Caswill (nee Wollen, later Emily Norton) was an interesting resident of Lawrence Grove from the early 1920s through to the 1960s.

This studio photo of Emily, Liz Cameron believes, must have been taken c.1930 when Emily would have been 46 years old. The name of the photographer is unknown. The Barton Hill Local History Group has also kindly provided some additional background about Emily who became a widely known and respected Bristol corset maker and fitter.

Emily Wollen was born in 1884, the first child of Albert and Emily Wollen living at 29, Charlton Street, St. Philips, Bristol. Her father Albert was a cabinet maker and he and his wife were to have four more children, although Kate, a daughter born in 1891 tragically died in infancy. Emily grew up in the Barton Hill district, the family having moved to 6, Bridge Street and she attended the first Board School that had been opened in Barton Hill, built in Jarvis Street in 1875. The school was a stone's throw from her home, just across the railway bridge. It would eventually become the Junior Technical School in the 1940s. On leaving school, she trained as a corset maker in one of the local corset factories, possibly Chappell & Allen which was within easy walking distance, and it is known that she also worked for some time at the Co-op corset factory in the Easton district.

During this period, the Wollen family moved again, settling this time at 2, Barrow Road, from which address Emily, now a fully trained and experienced corset maker was to set up her business. The shop was a small corner premises with a single large display window looking out onto the busy main road. There were always two or three mannequins in the window displaying traditional laced corsetry and there was an orange-coloured transparent blind that could be lowered to protect the merchandise from the effects of bright sunlight. A small bell was activated on the door when anyone entered the shop that would call Emily from her workroom at the back. Inside there was a large glass free-standing counter containing bras of all descriptions and other corsetry items. The wall behind the counter was completely covered by a large mahogany storage unit having 50 or so large pigeonholes in which Emily's stock of corsets were held. A side wall was covered with shelves piled high with white cardboard boxes containing yet more stock. The shop had an old fashioned ambience about it and it was spotlessly clean, with every item of brass work highly polished. Soon after she established her business, Emily's father died at the early age of 51 while Emily was only 27.

By this time Emily had met a young engineer, a local lad, Ernest Caswill whom she married in 1910 at the Russell Town Congregational Church, in Barton Hill. This gave a new impetus to the business with the shop facade soon displaying 'E J Caswill - Corsetiere'.

Emily continued developing her business at Barrow Road and in 1917 gave birth to a daughter Evelyn, her one and only child. Running the shop whilst caring for a new baby must have caused a few problems for Emily!

The following is a typical advertisement placed in local newspapers during this period:-

Western Daily Press

March 1924.

Madam Caswill (née E Wollen) Corset Specialist,

2 Barrow Road, Lawrence Hill, Bristol.

Any Corset made to order or copied.

A shock awaited Emily in 1937 when her husband Ernest died at the early age of 55 years. They had been married for 26 years.

Four years or so later in August 1941, Emily was married again, to Alfred Norton, a sewing machine representative, at the Methodist Church, Etloe Road, Westbury Park.

Later that same year, in October 1941, her daughter Evelyn married a young pharmacist, Thomas Jacobs, at the Parish Church of St. Peter, Henleaze.

By this time Emily was 57 years old whilst Alfred was 64. It would appear that Alfred had known Emily for some years, possibly calling at her shop premises in regard to her sewing machine requirements.

Liz Cameron believes that this photo of Emily and her daughter was taken in the garden of their home in Lawrence Grove. It may well have been taken in 1941 as they both married in that year, and the ages appear to be about right.

Unfortunately sad times were ahead for Emily. In 1946 her daughter Evelyn lost her life at the age of 29 years following the birth of her first child; a caesarean delivery leading to toxaemia (pre-eclampsia). The infant boy named Paul died at four days old in St. Brenda's Maternity Hospital, Clifton.

The following year in 1947 Emily's husband Alfred died; he was 70 years of age and they had been married for just 6 years.

Emily continued in business until about 1960 when she would have been 76 years old; she had been in business for almost 50 years!

She certainly was a very determined lady who continued her business through two world wars, the great Depression of the 1920s, and the tragedy of losing her daughter and grandson as well as two husbands!

In her final years she still looked after a number of her loyal customers and their corsetry needs from her home address at Lawrence Grove.

Emily finally passed away in 1967 at 83 years of age, having suffered a coronary thrombosis. By then it appears that she had moved away from Henleaze to Downend. Her brother Sidney Wollen was with her when she died. Her ashes were interred in the shrubbery area of Canford Cemetery, Bristol.

(1924 - 2013) AUDREY SEAL (NÉE BRIGINSHAW) - LONG-TERM RESIDENT

Audrey was born on 27th March 1924 and spent all of her early years, many of her married years and then her final years, in Henleaze. (Pictured here at the age of 86.)

She grew up very happily with doting parents who had been neighbours before their marriage. She started at a local school but wasn't happy there, until her grandfather offered to pay for her to go to St. Margaret's School, in Henleaze.

She thrived there, making many friends, some of whom she

remained close to, up to her death in April, 2013. St Margaret's encouraged a love of English literature, poetry and French, which the school excelled at. As a result her family was constantly amazed by the extent of her knowledge of literature, her ability to quote from it and her spelling. She was excellent at crosswords!

When she was 12, a sister, Joy, was born to her mother, who was by then 41.

In her teens (late 1930s) Audrey, second on the left tine the front row wearing a twin set, became a member of the Henleaze Congregational Church and its popular youth club.

She had drama and dance lessons and ice skated regularly with her father at the ice rink in Park Row. She loved dancing and joined the Glenda Maddocks School of Dance and Drama, one of whose alumni was Glynis Johns. Together, they performed at the Princess Theatre on Park Row, and the Hippodrome, many times. Audrey is in this 1934 photo, in the third row, fifth from the left wearing a brooch on her top and a hat on the side of her head.

Audrey acted on the stage at the church and was a Sunday school teacher. She was also a member of the Tennessee Grove tennis club – photo taken in 1940. Audrey is in the middle row, on the right next to Thelma Thompson.

The birth of Joy, illness, and subsequent onset of war, rendered her mother less able to care for the younger child, and Audrey took on the mantle of 'mother'. During the war, she and Joy slept together so that

Audrey could take her sister to the shelter in the reinforced garage beside their house in The Crescent. They became very close.

By this time, Audrey had become aware of the son of a neighbour in Henleaze Park Drive, Eric Seal, seven years older and training to become an accountant at the time. She continued her studies and then went to Clarks College, Clifton becoming a secretary just before the war.

Eric was posted to the North African desert for the duration of the war, but in 1944 Frank, his father, died suddenly and Eric was called home to take over the running of his cinema business. (At the time, the cinema was very important to morale, and people would visit them weekly or even more frequently). He was flown across the whole of war-torn Europe in a transport plane in what must have been a terrifying journey.

Upon his return Eric and Audrey met again and their future was sealed (!). Within a very short time they became engaged and were married on the 17th July 1945 at Henleaze Congregational church, just after the end of the war in Europe. Joy was a 9 year old bridesmaid and Audrey's other, older, bridesmaid and best friend, Thelma Thompson, remained a close friend to the end of her life.

In 1946, a daughter Carole was born. Audrey and Eric had bought a house in West Broadway, near to both sets of families, and continued to live there for 18 happy years. A second daughter, Wendy, was born in 1951.

By 2003, Audrey had started to find that glaucoma and macular degeneration were affecting her sight to the extent that very reluctantly, she had to make the decision to cease driving and move to Cote House on the Downs where she was initially content But on reflection, Cote was rather small and she felt she would be happier surrounded by more people, so she moved to Westfield House at St. Monica Trust.

Sadly, two hospital admissions at the end of 2012 took their toll and she very reluctantly gave up her independence and went into respite care; a hugely difficult decision for someone with such determination. After a fall, she was admitted to the BRI, and during her last days, she seemed relaxed and content. The care was wonderful and sensitive to her needs; neither Audrey nor her family could have asked for more. Sadly, Audrey died on April 6th 2013 (Eric's birthday) – a day which would have made her smile.

Audrey was a beautiful courageous friendly and loving woman. Her legacy to those left behind is the importance of creating a happy family, nurturing good friends and giving something back to society.

FOOTNOTE FROM CAROLE GOUGH (née SEAL):

'My maternal grandfather (photographed here during in the 1950s), Sydney Briginshaw died in 1984. He lived at 52 The Crescent. He was managing director of Cathedral Garage, now the City of Bristol College site – not far from the Bristol Central Library.

' Two of his most famous customers were Lord Wraxall (who lived in Tyntesfield House, now a National Trust property) and Cary Grant (whose mother lived in Linden Road, Westbury Park in her latter years. Cary would always come to visit her when in Bristol.)

'My paternal grandfather Frank Seal who died prematurely in his 50s in 1944, lived nearby at 49 Henleaze Park Drive. He had a keen interest in cinemas and was on the board of ABC Cinemas. As a chartered accountant and financier he was able to provide finance for several cinemas in Bristol including the Savoy at Shirehampton. He was also the BBC's financial commentator on Budget Day. He just had to walk along to the BBC from his office at 5 Whiteladies Road.'

The photograph of Frank Seal smoking a pipe is taken during the 1930s in his garden at Henleaze Park Drive.

'It was really thanks to my grandfathers who were good friends that my mother and father met!

(1928 - 1954) BRIAN ROBBINS - SCHOOLBOY & TIMBER MERCHANT

'Today is my 88th Birthday (18 February 2016) and one of my daughters has given me a copy of the Henleaze Book which I have found very fascinating. I lived at 30 Henleaze Gardens from birth in 1928 until my marriage in 1954, but with two absences, from 1940 to 1944 self-evacuated to Hope Cove in South Devon, and two and a half years in the Navy from November 1945 to April 1948.

'Your book has revived many memories, particularly the shops in Henleaze Road which seemed to fill a big part of my growing up. There are some omissions though, which you might like to investigate. One was St.Goar School, a thriving prep school run in my day before the war by Misses Peake and Rose, in a house I think 131 Westbury Road (near top of Falcondale Road), and which to my knowledge was still active for a good many years after the war. YMCA cricket club is mentioned, but not the rugby club which certainly ran between 1948 and 1958 when I was playing (badly!).

'There is mention of the 227th Scout Troop, which was a very thriving and active group, housed in the outbuildings of the Blind School you mentioned and later on in the Quarry as their HQ. Their neckerchiefs were green and brown, and as you mentioned it was Skipper Baldwin who was GSM in my day.

'One amusing memory I have is as a child watching the Orpheus Cinema being built and thinking the builders were making a big mistake with a flat wall for where the screen was going. Where was the space for the actors behind the screen?'

'When we returned from Hope Cove in Devon in September 1944, I started at Robbins Timber on 16th October that year and have worked there ever since apart from an exciting break in the Navy November 1945 to April 1948 and so am coming up to 72 years there!

'The Eastfield was the only 'watering hole' in the area, and the Downs Porter's Stores (affectionally known as Roleys) was a welcome alternative with only a beer licence, which suited me and my friends just fine.

'Apart from swimming, tennis and rugby, the St Peter's Youth Group met in the hall on Tuesday evenings, including one drama production of 'The Startled Saint' when as a leading character my wings dropped off! On Saturday nights there was always a dance in St. Peter's Hall from 7.30 to 11pm and there was a live band churning out the traditional mix of waltz, foxtrot and quickstep, in batches of three and with hokey kokey, conga and other frivolities before the traditional last waltz to end the evening. One of our favourite bands was Ken Lewis. It gave us an opportunity, as with the Youth Group, to meet girls, although I was somewhat shy of them.

'Life was good in Henleaze starting in April 1948 on demob. The war was over and almost forgotten even though rationing persisted. I started back at Robbins Timber, now working in the office rather than hitherto labouring in the saw mill, and life was full of fun. I joined Henleaze Lake Swimming Club that summer and the YMCA tennis club on Golden Hill. This led me to also joining the Rugby Club as tennis was rained off one Saturday afternoon and the Rugby was a man short! This was the start of a 10 year career in 'coarse' rugby. (Brian was Team Secretary during the 1953/4 season. This is confirmed by the Club card.)

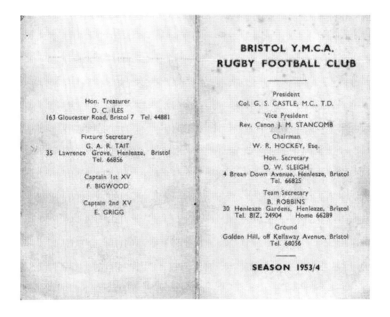

'Another feature of that time was night school, which I attended for four years studying Timber Technology at the Merchants Venturers' College in Unity Street. I finally graduated with a Higher Certificate and became a member of the Institute of Wood Science and entitled to the letters AIWSc which I never used.

'Cinema was an integral part of our lives, normally going once a week and the Orpheus in Northumbria Drive and the Carlton in Canford Lane serving us well. The library at the bottom of Falcondale Road also was regularly used. Dr Bayley on Westbury Road (between Cavendish and Brecon Roads) was a great doctor, and subsequently when we had moved to Backwell my wife still used him for her four pregnancies at St Brendan's Maternity Hospital by Clifton Parish Church.

'There were very few restaurants in those days, but I can recall King Alfred's Kitchen near Stokes Croft and I have a vivid memory of going out for a celebratory Coronation Dinner in the Mauretania at the bottom of Park Street at a cost of 10/6d (52p) each, the highest I had ever paid for a meal.

'May 14th 1951 was a red letter day for me when with a friend I went to the 96th North Somerset Show in Ashton Court (on a Whit Monday in those days), the sun shone and I met Jill Hobbs, and we immediately became an 'item'. We were married in August 1954 when she had completed teacher training college.

'I guess that is about all I can recall which may have been of interest. A Mr Powles and his son ran a garage in Cardigan Road which served me and my father well. He garaged his car there and I rented a garage in Henleaze Road when I eventually got a car in 1952. It was in the days before parked cars cluttered up all the Henleaze roads. On Bank Holiday weekends there was one continual queue of cars crawling along Henleaze Road, then over the Downs, past the Zoo and finally down Bridge Valley Road and the old swing bridges at Cumberland Basin.

'You could well say 'there have been some changes made!'

(1929 - 1965) OSWALD BROWN – DIRECTOR, FAMILY FIRM

In 1929 Oswald Frederick Leader Brown (1904 - 1977) moved from Clifton to Sunnyview, 18 Walliscote Avenue, Henleaze on his marriage on 18 September to Adele Mona Ryder Field (known as Mona).

Their only child, June, was born in 1930 and attended the local St Margaret's School, Henleaze from 1935 to 1941. Most of the children there were evacuated to Devon during WWII. However, June went on to finish her education at Clifton High School.

The photo from the June Miller (née Brown) collection shows the Harry Brown moored beside The Grove near the offices of T R Brown & Sons Ltd, by the Sailors' Home and opposite the River Police Station, now a restaurant.

June's great-grandfather Thomas Robert Brown, a master stevedore, started the family business as T R Brown & Son Ltd in 1860. He had realized the need for towage and lighterage in the Bristol Avon, the City

Docks and Avonmouth. The Bristol-based company also owned The Holms Sand and Gravel Company. Sand was subsequently dredged from the copious sandbanks in the Bristol Channel from 1912. T R Brown & Sons Ltd are perhaps best known to Bristolians for their dredgers, particularly the Harry Brown which was seen regularly making her way up and down the River Avon from the Bristol Channel to the City docks. T R Brown & Sons Ltd and Holms Sand & Gravel sand dredgers worked from Poole's Wharf in Hotwells until 1991.

It is traditional when launching a ship for a VIP to swing a champagne bottle at the bow. It is believed that this action brings good luck when the bottle is subsequently smashed on hitting the bows. In January 1950, June Miller felt privileged to be invited to perform this ceremony for the latest addition to the fleet of T R Brown & Sons Ltd. The Steep Holm had been built by Charles Hill & Sons, a major shipbuilder based in Bristol during the 19th and 20th centuries. Steep Holm should then have glided into the docks immediately following the ceremony but nothing happened! It was a really cold and frosty day and it appeared that the ship was reluctant to move down the slipway to enter the freezing water. Richard Hill, June's father Oswald Brown and her grandfather, Harry Brown peered anxiously over the dock wall to see what was causing the delay. Richard Hill, who was in charge of the launching, eventually ensured, after a great deal of pushing and heaving, that the Steep Holm slid perfectly into the dock and was finally launched – photo from the June Miller (née Brown) collection. This did not however take place until a full fifteen minutes after the ceremony. This unusual and unexpected delay made the national newspapers the next day!

In 1978 the re-established title Bristol Sand & Gravel Co. Ltd was used as a trading name for the joint venture between Bristol Dredging Company and the Holms Sand & Gravel Co. Ltd of Bristol to serve Bristol and Bridgwater. This venture continued until 1986 when both partners sold their interests in Bristol to,ARC Marine of Southampton.

(More details can be found in the excellent book – A Century of Sand Dredging in the Bristol Channel by Peter Gosson.)

June also added:

'All my family were christened Leader Brown which was their mother's surname – I am referring to the family of my grandfather Harry Brown and his 13 children.

'The fleet had these dredgers working in the Bristol Channel and elsewhere.

'Alwin (1922), Portway (1927), Sandholm (1932), Steep Holm (1950), Norwest (1955), Norstar (1961), Harry Brown (1962), Norleader (1967).'

Interestingly one of the dumb barges owned by the company was named the Henleaze.

'Several of my father's brothers also moved to Henleaze when they were young, a lovely place for the young.'

(1934 - 1947) KATHLEEN WALPOLE - AUTHOR & HEADMISTRESS

We have been unable to ascertain Kathleen Walpole's place of birth etc., but understand that she came from impoverished Irish gentry and that her mother was soon widowed.

The male population diminished considerably during WWI so there were few suitable men around to marry. Many girls, such as Miss Walpole, therefore embarked on careers.

Miss Kathleen Walpole served as Headmistress of Red Maids' School from 1934-1947. She steered the school through the difficult times of the Second World War.

The photo (courtesy of Red Maids) is of Kathleen Walpole relaxing among the sandbags. Note the china tea set on the windowsill. There were no mugs or teabags in those days!

After WWII Kathleen Walpole was wise enough to realise that Red Maids needed fresh blood to take on the post-war responsibilities of running this very successful school and that she herself needed to move on, as indeed she did to Wycombe Abbey School in Buckinghamshire (1948 – 1961).

Miss Walpole was an author and her historical works included:

"Emigration to British North America under the early Passenger Acts (1803-1842)" published in 1930.

She died in 1987.

(1935 - 1937) DEBORAH KERR - SCHOOLGIRL, ACTRESS & FILMSTAR

Deborah Kerr (1921 – 2007) was born in Helensburgh, Scotland. Her father, Captain Arthur Kerr-Trimmer, a civil engineer, was invalided out of the forces during the First World War and later developed tuberculosis. Her mother nursed her father and held the family together. When her husband died, she brought 14-year-old Deborah and her brother to live in Bristol where she struggled to make ends meet.

Deborah attended Northumberland House School until 1936 where her first acting opportunity was realised in the Mad Hatter's Tea Party.

She then attended the Hicks-Smale Drama School, run by her aunt Phyllis Smale, in Bristol before studying ballet at Sadler's Wells in 1937. She also worked for BBC Radio in Bristol in 1936 reading children's stories.

She married twice and had two daughters.

Over the years she received numerous Best Actress awards, but never an Oscar although she was nominated six times. However, in 1994 she was awarded an honorary Oscar and in 1997, the CBE.

Two of the films in which she appeared will be particularly remembered by many – The King and I with Yul Brynner (1956) and From Here to Eternity (1953) with Burt Lancaster. The highlights of these films, for many people, were her dance with Yul Brynner and her steamy scene on the beach with Burt Lancaster.

(1940s) PATSY PARRY - MEMORIES OF HER WELLINGTON HILL WEST FAMILY HOME

In 1996 Patsy wrote from her home in Paignton, Devon to local Harbury Road resident Michael Stephenson. Here are some extracts:

'I was absolutely delighted to receive your letter this morning, and the photos of the Harbury Road shops. How very kind of you.

'Now where shall I start? My father (Gordon Parry) was a very well-known builder before the war. Harbury Road was just a field and he built and developed it but only the shops on the right going up, not the Co-op side, as the ground over there had a problem and he always said they should not build between the hairdresser (Mr Davies) and the Co-op.

'Our house was 161 Wellington Hill West and our side garden was in Harbury Road. Gordon, my father, made a gate in the fence for the Bunkers to come in and share our air-raid shelter, which he built underground with three tons of concrete on top.

'Our leaded light windows were a wedding present to my parents, and they were above the front door and the side panels. I think the new owners have put a door on the porch. So with luck the window should still be inside. (The leaded stained glass panels are still there as can be seen from this photo courtesy of Libby Bloor.)

'It broke my heart to leave our house and the lead lights. My father kept a lovely garden, with full moon beds and half moon beds of geraniums and wallflowers etc. A Mr and Mrs Wales bought the house from us and I believe they stayed there until their death. I would love a photo of MY leaded lights.

'If you do go and knock on the door tell the people you have written to me, and as I spent a very happy childhood in the house I would love a photo of the window.

(Photo now kindly submitted by the present owners of Patsy's former home.)

'I have not been up to Bristol for a few years as my father died at just over 50 years old and my mother became ill, so I have nursed her for a few years and she died last year. My mother would have loved the photos of the shops. We of course knew the owners so well, as they all bought them off my father, and people were so friendly in those days.

'I was born in the year when the Second World War started. My father built a very large chicken house at the top of the garden and he would give eggs to all the neighbours, and also things from the greenhouse. Dear Mrs Bunker, the grocer, used to make up a parcel of currants and things when they could get them and she used to put the parcel on top of the chicken house. Happy Days!

'My father built a lovely house on the corner of Owen Grove and Holmes Grove for the Baileys who had a shop at 107-113 Gloucester Road. It was pre-war and, I think, it had a wrought iron staircase. But Gordon always said that it needed more ground, but they wanted it built there! He built a lot around Bristol, then the war came and he had to join up, so that was the end to the building trade.'

In 1952 Gordon Parry wanted to restart his building business in Bristol, but the only licences available then were for council housing. (In 1939 he had employed more than 100 men in the Bristol area over three private housing sites but, like other building companies, had to close down at the start of WWII.) So the family left for Devon where they hoped to buy some ground for building. As a temporary measure, until Gordon could obtain a licence to build private houses, they ran a hotel. Unfortunately his health deteriorated and he died when he was only in his early 50s, before he could obtain the necessary building licence for private housing.

Patsy is a St Ursula's Old Girl and remembers Sister Cecilia well. The old girls held a reunion in May 2016.

(1941 - 1995) JILL SIMS (NÉE ATTFIELD) MBE - ST MARGARET'S SCHOOLGIRL & GOVERNOR'S SECRETARY, H. M. PRISON, BRISTOL

Jill, the eldest of three girls, lived for the first part of her life in Seymour Road, off Stapleton Road, Bristol. During the Bristol Blitz, she had taken refuge with her mother and baby sister in a nearby shelter when their house, a three storey property, received a direct hit. Although a very young child at that time, Jill clearly remembers the injured and some dead bodies being brought into their shelter. She was so frightened then that she completely unpicked the hem of her dressing gown and bit all of her nails down as far as she could. Her father was away on secret work at that time.

The family moved to Laurie Crescent in Henleaze and for a short time Jill also lived with her grandparents in the flat over their Mounstevens' bakery in Ashley Down. She has very happy memories of that time and can recall her cupboard-sized bedroom there and the smell of freshly baked bread coming from the rear of the shop each morning. The family also lived in one of the Victorian cottages in Kellaway Avenue opposite the former Kellaway Arms. Jill's maternal grandparents, the Mountstevens, provided the funds for her to attend St Margaret's School in Henleaze Park plus additional singing, drama and elocution lessons. Jill found the discipline strict and two of the teachers, Miss Bell and Miss Campbell, quite frightening. However she enjoyed her time there. Jill had been born with a boy soprano voice and singing was her favourite lesson. She also excelled in tennis and, despite breaking several racquets, she played for the school team. Hedley Goodall, the talented drama tutor, developed in Jill a lifelong interest in the performing arts. Jill recalled singing in harmony at home with one of her sisters who was a lower soprano whilst their Mother played the piano.

Jill's family were not well off and so it was necessary for her to leave

St Margaret's School when she was 15 years old to provide them with some additional income. For just over a year she attended Simpson's Secretarial College on nearby Horfield Common to obtain a qualification as a shorthand typist which enabled her to quickly find a job with Radio Rentals in Zetland Road. Jill's Grandmother then bought her a bike so she could travel from home in Henleaze to work more easily. However, on the first day Jill tried cycling to work, at the Zetland Road junction there was a policeman directing traffic. When he beckoned Jill on, she cycled up behind his back to pass him more easily. He was then engaged with other traffic and did not realise what she was doing. He took a step back and ended up on the floor with Jill and her bike. Needless to say Jill decided not to cycle to work from then on. Jill also held several more jobs after her time with Radio Rentals. Two of the companies went bankrupt. Her next job was with the Bradford Equitable Building Society which was located on the City Centre. In those days there were no shops nearby in which to buy food. Fortunately, Jill was able to catch a bus part of the way home during her lunch hour to enable her to have a meal. Jill grew very thin with all this exercise and was advised to look for a job nearer home.

Jill's Mother subsequently saw a position for a shorthand typist that was advertised at HMP Bristol. It meant taking an exam for the Civil Service but Jill passed and was accepted.

On 5 April 1952 Jill Sims, 19 years old, walked through the gate at HMP Bristol to start her first day's work there. She remained at Horfield for 42½ years of continuous service.

Jill was the first woman to work at HMP Bristol, and remained as the only female member of staff for more than a decade. She started as a shorthand secretary to the Governor but, during her career, covered most jobs on the administrative side of the prison. She was also involved in court work for much of her time there.

The Prison Service Jill joined back in 1952 was one, she recalled, that was much stricter in discipline than today. Inmates had to turn and face the wall when Jill walked past. When the death penalty was still in force until 1963, Jill was given half a day off whenever an execution took place but had to type up the hospital report afterwards.

Jill served with generations of officers from the same families, as fathers were often followed by sons. She has a lot of friends in other prison establishments with whom she keeps in touch. She does however miss the humour and her colleagues. Although the work was hard at times, it was very rewarding. When Jill retired in 1995 she was awarded the MBE and also the Imperial Service Order Medal for her long and outstanding service.

The Imperial Service Order was established by King Edward VII in August 1902. It was awarded on retirement to the administration and clerical staff of the Civil Service throughout the British Empire for long and meritorious service. See https://en.wikipedia.org/wiki/Imperial_Service_Order

An MBE is an award given by the Queen to an individual for outstanding service to the community or local 'hands on' service. The definition of MBE is Member of the Most Excellent Order of the British Empire. See http://www.awardsintelligence.co.uk/ Jill's final comments on her career 'Behind Bars': "I've loved it. I've no regrets."

Since her retirement Jill has regularly given presentations to local care and nursing homes as well as Probus. Her two subjects are Humorous Poetry and 'My Life behind Bars'. She considers her presentation successful if she can make the audience laugh, particularly any who have Alzheimer's disease or dementia. She makes no charge for her presentations but does ask for donations to her favourite charity, the Great Western Air Ambulance Service.
http://www.greatwesternairambulance.com/

(1942 - 1964) PAT BRAIN - RESIDENT

2014 - Extracts from emails:

'I only came across the Henleaze Blog a couple of weeks ago and thoroughly enjoyed reading up on my old neighbourhood.

'I lived on Oakwood Road from 1942-1959 and then towards the end of Hill View from 1959 to 1964 when I left for Canada.

'I believe I attended St Ursula's from 1948-1950 before switching to La Retraite in Clifton. I recall the Torpy twins being there at that time. My brother Adrian attended Claremont School and then Henleaze Junior School and I well remember my mother being impressed with 'Mr. Charles' (the first Headmaster of HJS).

'A rainy Field Day at St. Ursula's in 1948. I am the very elegant one sitting on the left end of the bench!

'We lived very close to the Bristol Royal School for the Blind (demolished in 1970 to make way for new housing) and I well remember seeing groups of pupils walking up Henleaze Road. Behind their wall along Henleaze Road was a large field with a donkey (known as Happy).

The school had a huge bonfire on Guy Fawkes' night and we used to see it growing steadily bigger as the day drew closer. Anyone in the neighbourhood could attend and watch Guy Fawkes burning and enjoy the fireworks. Although the children could not see, they could feel the warmth on their faces and hear the fireworks and certainly enjoyed themselves. At some point the school installed an outdoor in-ground swimming pool and my friend and I were fortunate enough to be among the few outsiders able to swim there each summer for a small fee.

'Badock's Wood used to be a great place catch tadpoles and to explore, although a little dark and scary! (See weblink: http://www.fobw.org.uk/) I can't imagine parents letting their kids go there alone at such young ages as we did. I belonged to Henleaze Lake Swimming Club for a couple of years and that was a great place to meet the boys.'

Henleaze Lake 2015 showing the diving board, photo courtesy of Julie Kaye. For more details of the club see: http://www.henleazeswimmingclub.org/

'We frequented the Library in Westbury-on-Trym, next to Canford

Park – a nice little walk down Water's Lane and past the cinema if I remember rightly. (Carlton Cinema in Canford Lane was demolished in 1960. It was replaced by Carlton Court, a shopping precinct.)

'Saturday mornings were often spent at the Orpheus Cinema's children's show, watching cartoons and cowboy movies, ending with a serial, ensuring we would be back the following week. (The Orpheus Cinema, built in 1937 was demolished in the 1970s to make way for a Waitrose complex. However, thanks to public outrage Waitrose included a new cinema on this site.)

'We attended the Sacred Heart Catholic Church and I well remember the Newman Hall being built (1962) and people being able to go there after the 12 o'clock Mass for a drink – times were changing! Our Youth Club met in Newman Hall on Sunday evenings, and Scouts and Girl Guides during the week.'

Sacred Heart Catholic Church and Newman Hall, 2013.

(These 2013 photos courtesy of local photographer Julie Kaye.)

(1943 - 1962) RICHARD WALKER - HENLEAZE RESIDENT

1953 – Richard Walker aged 10.

Many thanks to Richard for submitting these family photos and the following memories of Henleaze.

'I found the Henleaze Book an extremely interesting read as I once lived at No 63 Lakewood Crescent, a house my parents moved into during the 1930s from their rented flat in Clifton. They moved soon after it was built and rented it until they left again to move back to Clifton in 1962. I was born in 1943 and grew up in this house, not leaving it until I was 19 years old.

'We rented the house from Ivor Voke, our landlord. I recall with some clarity that every rent day, he drove a really posh Humber Super Snipe car at a time when hardly anyone had cars, it was his habit to knock the front door handle with great force, there then being no doubt whatsoever that it was he at the door for the rent. My mother kept the 'rent book' in a bureau that stood just inside the hall. I think the rent was 10 shillings every fortnight. He had an extremely loud voice and would bellow "Good day Mrs Walker, your rent please."

'I learned from the Henleaze Book that Mr Voke was the architect; well, our house must have been one of the cheaper designs, as it had no bathroom. The bath was in the kitchen and the house had a separate outside toilet, and there was a coal scullery built into the wall located under the stairwell at the back door. The kitchen was equipped with a then-standard gas oven, and a floor-standing zinc gas boiler for clothes-washing and for filling the bath. The hot water for the bath was transferred to it by filling saucepans from the tap on the boiler. The bath itself was covered with a large wooden plank that had to be lifted off and set aside every time anyone used the bath. There was no central heating or hot water except from an Ascot gas water heater over the sink in the kitchen. There was also a larder built into the living room that had a very small window with one of the panes replaced with metal gauze for ventilation. The coal fireplaces were set across the corner of the two reception rooms. There was no heating at all upstairs.

'The windows were metal Crittall type and all of them rusted very badly. The house had three bedrooms, a box room and two others. In those days Lakewood Road and Lakewood Crescent were lit by gas street lights, and at every other street light there was a 'pig bin' into which everyone was expected to place their household food scraps to help feed the nation's pigs. Now that's austerity! Rationing was still in force and my mother would shop at the Harbury Road Coop Store and collect the "Divi" points you would earn when shopping in the Coop and quoting your "Divi" number which I can still remember to this day.

'Despite all of these shortcomings it was my home and we all (my parents and two brothers) had great affection for it. The house is still there, now much improved, I guess. My two brothers were 10 years older than me; their names are David and Michael (sadly David has since passed away) and Michael now lives in Staple Hill.

1950s - Front room fireplace – 63 Lakewood Crescent.

'Florence Esther (Flo) Walker was my mother, seen looking out of the front bedroom window. The photo was taken in the early 1950s. She would have been in her 50s when this image was taken. It's a bit of an odd angle but I quite like it. Flo lived until she was 89. She was born on 24 December, 1904.

Coronation 1953 - Lakewood Road and 1953 Coronation tea party, - Lakewood Crescent.

'This group of friends are sitting on a wall in Lakewood Road. The house in the background is No 61 Lakewood Crescent with my house No 63 just out of shot. The road sign said 'No Through Road for Motor Vehicles'. The boys' names are from left to right (sitting) John Smith, John Bright, I can't remember the next boy's name, but I'm sure it's Gordon's brother, then I think Peter Young. Standing at the back are

Gordon Touffery (not too sure of the surname spelling), then myself Richard Walker (age about 10) and the little girl; I'm afraid I can't recall her first name but her surname was Perry.

1950s – The Badock's Wood end of Lakewood Road, showing what was known as 'The Terrace', the small road leading off to the right.

(1946 - 2012) MAURICE TORPY, WWII HERO & CONSULTING ENGINEER

Michael, one of his sons, begins:

'I have been interested in history all my life and would like to think that my parents' time at 8 Carmarthen Road was remembered.

'My father was reluctant to talk of the war and my brother and I knew only a few snippets, but I felt that given the fact Dad had been an Officer, been in so many POW camps and survived the war, records must exist. I visited the National Archives and was rewarded to find a two page manuscript report written by my father when he was de-briefed on his return home, together with a report by the British Commandant of Stalag Luft 3A on the forced march from the camp, and to see Dad's name in a list of Officers and men who went missing on the march.

'My father was a modest man and wouldn't consider himself to be famous, but fortunately for us he was a survivor; anyhow this is one resident of Henleaze's war time experiences.'

This is some of the information about Maurice's war time experiences, compiled by Michael Torpy and his brother David in 2014.

'Our father, Maurice Torpy, first trained for WWII in Everton, Scotland, during which time he flew down to Bristol (no parachute) to be married in April 1941. He was posted to Manby, Lincs, as an armaments officer. Then after a few months, at the end of June, he went to Salisbury Plain and from there to a ship at Liverpool for North Africa via Durban. Shortly after arriving in North Africa he was captured, two weeks before the birth of his twin sons on the 24th February 1942. He escaped across the desert from Benghazi on the night of 28/29 Jan 1942. The enemy had them trapped but some evaded the Germans and got clear; walked east making for Tobruk until captured by German patrol somewhere SW of Derna on 11 Feb 1942. He was listed missing presumed dead for two years and Iris received a widow's pension.

'He was a POW in the desert and then in Italy and spoke warmly of the Italians. The Vatican traced him. Mother never got his missing officer's salary for those 2 years. When Italy fell, he was rail-trucked to Germany.

'This is a copy of Stalag Luft 3 ID card of our Father Maurice (aged 27) taken in November 1943.

'He helped spread sand in preparation for the Wooden Horse escape from this POW camp and survived the killings after the mass breakout. As the Germans retreated from the advancing Russians, the prisoners were force-marched on the Long March from Stalag Luft III. Maurice collapsed in the snow at the roadside, left for dead and was last seen on 29 January, 1945. He somehow survived and was taken into a French POW camp at Muskau where he was medically treated.

'He was then put in Stalag Luft 3A. This was liberated by the Russians on the 21 April 1945; the Germans had just fled. Dad was trucked to Halle in Belgium from where he was airlifted to the UK on the 28 May 1945.

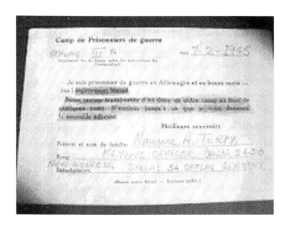

'This is a copy of the postcard received by our Mother, Iris in 1945 proving Dad was alive and had survived the forced march from Stalag Luft 3.

'My mother Iris said that his comrades who had escaped the march via Norway were ringing her to ask what happened to Maurice. She saw a fellow officer in the street in Bristol and both were too afraid to speak to ask what had happened. Then Dad phoned her from Belgium. He said he owed his survival to his greatcoat (pictured on his ID card). This was treasured in our home for many years; he said it saved his life. (It was worn by son David in the school CCF.)

'He was demobbed to a wife and twin boys aged four that he had never seen. He had lost all his teeth. Iris had not seen him for five years - since one night on his way to Liverpool.

'Dad had a favourite meal of peanut butter, marmalade, and cheese sandwich – like a Red Cross food parcel.'

In the summer of 1946, Iris and her husband Maurice, a former RAF POW who had survived the notorious Stalag Luft 111 prison camp, moved into 8 Carmarthen Road. They raised a family of six children who all attended St Ursula's Convent; Christopher and David, Michael, Clare, Catherine and Mary.

'Our Mother Iris (aged 29) taken in the summer of 1948 in a friend's garden in Henleaze, with Micky in the pram.

'Maurice, started his own consulting engineers' business when back in Henleaze, Maurice A Torpy & Partners, specialising in heating and ventilating hospitals. He enjoyed playing cricket for Southmead Hospital cricket club. He became a Governor of St Ursula's and spent many years helping the school.

'Dad always kept in touch with Ron Gray from Australia who had been his friend in the camp and probably helped save his life. The Grays came to England in the late 80s and stayed with dad and mum. Dad never really talked about his POW experiences, but for a brief period in 1945 managed to keep a diary. He certainly never glamourised it, but rather had nightmares, especially at the end of his life.

'He passed away in April 1993. Iris survived him into her 93rd year at No 8, cared for by her family.

'Iris Torpy (nee Franklin), our mother, was the oldest resident of Carmarthen Road. She died on 29 October 2012 at the age of 92. Iris had been a nurse at St Mary's hospital and met her husband, Maurice whilst nursing his mother. They married in 1941.'

(1950s - 1970s) ANDREA BAMFORD (NÉE WILLIAMS) – MY EARLY YEARS IN HENLEAZE

'I was born and christened Andrea Williams in 1955. My brother Robert was born in 1958 and then my sister Karen in 1960. I am pictured here with my Mum, Dorothy outside the historic row of terraced properties known as Dorset Villas. Our home was no 2. I have always had an interest in older buildings and their history, probably as a result of living in this area in my youth.

'We had a great childhood and were able to play in the waste ground at the rear of the villas at the end of the drive, behind the wooden gates in Eastfield Terrace. This drive led to the old stable and garage where I assume a carriage was kept at one time.

'Our dad rented part of this property as his workshop (he was an engineer and carpenter) and above this was a small upstairs room in which, at one time, he used to develop pictures. There was a small area where we hung out our washing at the very end of the drive, and for many years next to this was "the bombed building"; our name for what may have been a building at some point. This was where we played, built dens, put on shows for our parents and had annual bonfire parties with neighbours etc., etc; such freedom!

'Another 'playground' was the old quarry across the road. I am sure we weren't meant to be there, but it was wonderful for building dens and having adventures! In the summer we swam in the outdoor pool in the grounds of the School for the Blind (across the other side of the Henleaze Road dual carriageway) where we were members. We also had swimming lessons on Friday evenings after school at Bristol North Pool on Gloucester Road, now closed. We used to walk there from Henleaze School with mum pushing my sister Karen in a pushchair up what I remember were a couple of big hills! (Probably Kings Drive in Bishopston.)

'I attended Henleaze Junior School from September 1963 – July 1967 and kept all my reports (eight in total – two a year!) I think this photo was taken in my second year. (1964-1965.) Mrs Scannell was the teacher. I am third from the right, front row - Andrea Williams. Third from the left front row is Caroline Farley, I believe. After 55 years all the other names have been forgotten.

'We were members of St Peter's Church. My brother, Robert, was in the choir for some years and we all attended Sunday school, Brownies, Guides, Cubs and Scouts.

'Dad was a Cub Scout leader for many years and he helped to build the Cub/Scout hut in the corner of the old quarry; this is where my husband and I had our wedding reception in April 1976 after our wedding at St Peter's. (Baldwin Lodge was opened here in 1975 for the 227th St Peter's Scout Group. No meeting was cancelled during the eight years of construction work which cost £6,500.)

'One of my favourite things about our involvement with the church was the seemingly regular jumble sales in the church hall. We had the entire jumble in our houses in piles and I just loved going through it all and then helping out at the sales! I got some wonderful treasures. I still get teased about my fondness for old fabric, wood and rusty metal! We had lovely Christmas parties at St Peter's church hall, I presume with the Sunday school, and I had a part in a play when I was about 10 or 11 which was performed there.

'My ballet lessons were in the church hall and when I reached teenage years, Saturday night was band night!

'Some of these things I had forgotten about, but it is funny how a few old photos bring it all back! When we were quite young the church held some sort of fete in the car park at the front and in the surrounding grounds.

'I have such lovely memories of Henleaze.

'My brother Robert and I both live in Surrey nowadays. We have decided that one day we will go back and walk around for a while to see how much Henleaze has changed! Any history on the Henleaze area always grabs my attention.'

1950s - 1990s) ELAINE HORSEMAN - TEACHER & BEST-SELLING AUTHOR

Thanks to Andrea Bamford (nee Williams) who lived in Dorset Villas, Henleaze, from the 1950s to 1970s, these memories have come to light.

Andrea's mother, Dorothy Williams had become friendly with a neighbour, Elaine Horseman from Cheriton Close, who was a teacher at Henleaze Junior School when Andrea attended.

Here is an extract from the panoramic photo of Henleaze Junior School taken in 1957 (courtesy of http://www.htempest.co.uk/about-tempest-photography.htm). Mrs. Horseman is in the centre of the picture, to the right of Mr. Burgess.

When Elaine Horseman, left Henleaze Junior School in the early 1960s she changed careers and became the author of three children's books. They centre on five children in an old Victorian house and their experiences with a book of magic spells. According to Wikipedia, she was 'She was the second of nine children and grew up in a house very like the Hubbles'. https://en.wikipedia.org/wiki/Elaine_Horseman

Her three books are:

Hubble's Bubble. 1964

The Hubbles' Treasure Hunt. 1965

The Hubbles and the Robot. 1968

An entry in Henleaze Junior School log for its 25th exhibition (7-11 November, 1977) shows Elaine as one of their guests, but gave no indication of her current role then as a well known children's author.

This is a quote on Amazon from Carole J. Walker on January 7, 2015:

'Elaine Horseman was the J.K. Rowling of her day. Book ingredients included: witchcraft, candlesticks, three English children and a mouse. I read this as a child in the 1960s and never forgot it. The name Alaric charmed me so I looked it up. He was a King of the Visigoths.'

Elaine was married to Leslie Horseman and had two sons, Stephen and Christopher. She died in Bristol in 1999.

Does anyone remember Elaine Horsemen at Henleaze Junior School during the late 1950s and early 1960s? Does anyone recall reading her books?

(1952 - 1957) TOM GRAVENEY - CRICKETER

Much has been written about cricketer Tom Graveney (1927 – 2015) but this offering covers just the years 1952 – 1957 when he was living in Henleaze. When Tom and local girl Jackie married in 1952 they stayed with his in-laws in one of the two former lodges of Henley Grove Mansion which was demolished in 1967. Both lodges survived, but this particular one is now known as 132 Henleaze Road. On the death of Sid Brookman, Tom's father-in-law, they moved up to Winchcombe with Jackie's mother to be nearer Jackie's sister who ran the George Pub at Winchcombe. Tom kindly sent us the picture of their marriage in 1952.

1953 - Tom was named as one of the five Wisden Cricketers of the Year.

1953-54 - A score of 92 in Trinidad was his main contribution in the classic England tour of the Caribbean.

1955 - The following winter he was selected only twice in the winning series in Australia. At least triumph came at the end of the tour when he made a century in the fifth Test at Sydney, his only 100 against the Aussies.

1956-57 - He was not chosen for the tour of South Africa even though he had just made 2,397 runs in the summer, which remained his best total score.

1957 – Back in the England team, he followed a duck against the West Indies at Lord's with 258 at Trent Bridge, which was to be his highest first-class score. In England's third victory of that series he made 164 at The Oval in the final Test.

1968 - Tom captained England only once at the age of 41 against Australia at Headingley. He was also awarded the OBE that same year.

2005 – Tom became the 200th president of the MCC.

Tom Graveney played cricket for Gloucestershire and was one of England's finest batsmen,

"He was a courteous class act, delighting watchers with his masterly batting and bowling."

Many books have been written about him but this particular one gives a good insight into this unique and memorable man: Tom Graveney: A Biography by Christoper Sandford.

Tom Graveney kindly sent this photo of himself and Jackie on their wedding day in 1952 for the author to include in information relating to themselves and Henleaze.

(1957 - 2007) ARTHUR MILTON - CRICKETER/FOOTBALLER

I contacted Tom Graveney in 2008 to enquire about the years that he had lived in Henleaze as I wanted wish to include him in a presentation at Henleaze Library that April as one of the Famous Henleaze Folk. He said that Arthur Milton was more worthy of a place than he was! However both of them are now included! Unbeknown to me, Joan Milton, Arthur's widow had actually attended that April, 2008 presentation at the Library.

In the summer of 2014 I made contact with Joan Milton, who still lives in Henleaze. She was subsequently kind enough to grant me access to many photographs of Arthur and also his biography by his good friend Mike Vockins "Arthur Milton: Last of the Double Internationals."

Arthur's numerous friends included Denis Compton (like Arthur he was also a Brylcreem Boy – these were normally famous sportsman who endorsed the Brylcreem range of hair care products during the 1950s), Joe Mercer, Tony Brown, Andy Wilson, Don Oakes, Jimmy Logie, Barrie Meyer, Peter Richardson, Paul Fisher, David Shepherd, David Green, John Claughton, Denis Scanlan, Tom and Ken Graveney, Dougie Tucker (his dog racing friend) and of course Mike Vockins the biographer of "Arthur Milton: Last of the Double Internationals" published in 2011 by Sports Books Ltd.

Much has been written about England footballer and cricketer Arthur Milton. As this book is about residents of Henleaze, we have covered some highlights from the 50 years (1957 – 2007) when Arthur lived in Henleaze with his family.

Arthur was one of only 12 men who played cricket AND football for England.

1957 – Joan, Arthur's wife, found them a house in Henleaze, Bristol and they moved in on their fourth wedding anniversary on 22 August. They had three sons Robert, David and Richard.

1958 - First Test cap v New Zealand at Headingley in his 10th season as a professional. A debut century earned him a place on the Ashes tour. He became the first Gloucestershire player to score a century in his first Test since W G Grace in 1880.

1965 - His highest score (170) v Sussex at Cheltenham.

1967 - His best summer – more than 2,000 runs and 39 catches.

1968 - Appointed as County Captain. Under Arthur's leadership they reached the Gillette Cup quarter-final at Trent Bridge. They had never progressed beyond the third round in previous years. Arthur gave up captaincy after this one season as he did not enjoy it.

1972 - Scored his final, 52nd century (117) v Worcester.

1974 - Arthur's playing career ended against Yorkshire at Harrogate.

1975 – 1978 - He was mentor and coach to the University of Oxford's cricketers.

1978 – 1988 - Arthur then met, by chance, in Westbury-on-Trym a cricket fan, Cyril Wood, who told him there was a vacancy in the Post Office. Cyril was a local cricketer and a postmaster who looked after the local sorting office. Arthur decided that this new career would keep him active and soon he was delivering letters for the Sneyd Park/Stoke Bishop round. It was ten years he really enjoyed and the bonus was meeting a lot of people during that time. "It got me out of myself," he said. The Post Office arranged a retirement party from him and gave him two excellent prints of local scenes by Frank Shipsides. He was able to see his three sons during this time whilst they were still living at home.

1988 - Their first granddaughter, Stephanie was born on Arthur's 60th birthday. This was the year he retired as a postman. After that he took on a newspaper round in the Rockleaze and Stoke Bishop areas and later even continued to manage it himself after the local store decided to stop providing the service

*

When Arthur retired from his paper round he gave several of the friends he had made during this work a signed copy of this photo.

2001 – Through his paper round Arthur also met Donald Shell, the warden of Wills Hall. In due course Donald was amazed to learn that Arthur had been such a sporting star. He invited him to be Guest of Honour at a Sports Formal. The newly-appointed Vice-Chancellor, Eric

Thomas, attended. He was very impressed with Arthur on this first visit. Donald recalled that it was one of the best moments as warden of the hall. "Around a hundred of the most privileged students were hearing a piece of wisdom delivered by someone possessed of immense natural authority." The students were enthralled. Thereafter Arthur and Joan became regular guests and welcome visitors to the Hall.

It reads: *'Just a boy, still a paper boy. Be well and happy. Best wishes'* Arthur

Retirement – Arthur was now able to spend more time at home with Joan, when not at Eastville or Long Ashton. They went to the Proms at the Albert Hall, supported the Bristol Old Vic and Bristol Hippodrome and attended concerts at the Colston Hall.

Arthur joined a team of Observers for the TCCB – the Test & County Cricket Board, a far-sighted idea by Ted Dexter, and stayed for about three years.

2002 - University of Bristol gave Arthur an honorary MA.

He had previously delivered the newspapers to the Common Room!

Arthur gave a copy of this photo to local residents Jane and John Golding, when he retired from his Stoke Bishop paper round.

2006 - Arthur phoned Mike Vockins about a possible biography. He had received offers over the years, but decided he could only pursue with Mike's help. The completed book contains some fascinating information as well as many previously unseen photographs. The book is a true inspiration to all budding sportsmen and sportswomen. It is so refreshing to learn about many interesting and famous participants and their achievements in the days before money became so important in football and cricket.

The book - Arthur Milton: the Last of the Double Internationals - was published in May 2011 and is available on-line at various outlets including this one on Amazon: https://www.amazon.co.uk/Arthur-Milton-Last-Double-Internationals/dp/1907524037/ref=aag_m_pw_dp?ie=UTF8&m=AHRB2OK2Q2YCL

Mike Vockins, its compiler, was secretary of Worcestershire CCC for thirty years, retiring in 2001. He then managed international tours abroad and also became a popular speaker and lecturer.

Arthur continued to enjoy golf until the last eight or nine months of his life when he had a mini stroke

2007 - Arthur died on 25th April.

Joan Milton was kind enough to spend time and to give me access to so many wonderful memories of her husband, Arthur. I thank her and also Mike Vockins for creating such an interesting book on this great and unique man.

(1958 - 1962) ALTHEA MAY HARRIGAN - NOW KNOWN AS PETA HARRIGAN COLE. SCHOOLGIRL FROM THE CARIBBEAN

Peta and her two brothers were sent from the British Virgin Islands to Bristol by their father to obtain a British education. Her brothers lived with an uncle in Southmead and attended Clifton College as day boys, but Peta boarded at St. Margaret's School, Henleaze. Two of the former pupils there have very strong memories of her.

Boarder and school friend Mary Weekes wrote:

'Althea May Harrigan known by all, apart from Miss John and other staff, as Pete or Peta, arrived at St Margaret's not long after I did. We were drawn to each other due to shared feelings of homesickness. She was from Tortola in the British Virgin Islands. Her parents deemed it important for her to leave her home in the Caribbean and to come to England to have an English education. She stayed with her uncle in Southmead during school holidays.

'I am not sure that I appreciated then the fact that it must have been a huge culture shock for her, and I certainly had no awareness of race or colour issues. She was just Peta. She was a girl of similar age and she was a boarder and we liked each other.

'I was fascinated by the way she needed to care for her hair and skin, explaining to me that there was insufficient sunshine to maintain good condition so she used coconut oil liberally and a tight stocking on her hair at night to keep it in control.

'Her mother used to send her parcels containing the aforementioned coconut oil but also exotic fruits and preserves, the likes of which we had never heard, let alone seen. She shared her guava jam with me.

'We both slept in 'Concorde' dorm together with Sue Thomas and shared many wheezes and secrets that will always remain so! We made a point of helping Sue Thomas escape the wrath of staff on a regular basis. We were firm friends for all of the time we were together.'

Day girl and school friend, Elizabeth Popham (Poppie) wrote:

'Althea to staff, and Pete to her day girl class mates, she was just who she was, a kind, very intelligent girl, and we were friends.

'Her brother Derek was a day boy at Clifton College at the same time and stayed with his uncle.'

Over the years both Mary and Elizabeth had lost track of Peta, but thanks to additional research and the internet we finally ascertained that she was living in the USA. Elizabeth had written to her after we had her address and following that letter Elizabeth reported that:

"Her son Derek sent an email just after Christmas 2015 which contained the following information from Peta:"

'What a pleasant surprise to hear from my pastor that you have been trying to contact me. Please send me details of your proposed e-book and any information you may have about Mary Weekes. This is really exciting after such a long time. Look forward to hearing from you. Happy New Year'!

Peta does not use email which is why we heard from her son, after initially being in touch with her pastor. Fortunately there was one book still in stock of the limited edition of "St Margaret's: Memories, Musings & Merriment" which Elizabeth sent to Peta. NB There are copies of the e-book edition available via Amazon if anyone would like one. https://www.amazon.co.uk/ST-MARGARETS-MEMORIES-MUSINGS-MERRIMENT-ebook/dp/B00UG6VTB2/

Mary Weekes kindly provided the photo of Peta taken in the British

Virgin Islands in 1962

(1964 - 1982) JOHN ZIMAN - PHYSICIST & HUMANIST

John Ziman (1925 – 2005) was appointed professor of theoretical physics at the University of Bristol in 1964. The first blue plaque in Henleaze was placed on the wall of his former home, Eastfield Lodge, in 2008 to commemorate his work. For further information see:
https://en.wikipedia.org/wiki/John_Ziman#cite_note-18

This book looks at John from the perspective of one of his daughters, Kate when he lived in Henleaze with his first wife, Rosemary and their four children. Many thanks to Kate for giving us access to her family photo collection.

´Until dad died I never realised the impact he had on so many people. He was a kind and gentle man and had the ability to make you feel special. A present or postcard would be chosen with such care. The stories he would read would capture the imagination and you could not wait for him to read the next chapter. (Photo taken of John sat on a garden chair in the early 1980s.)

'The garden was his and mum's pride and joy. There was always a colourful selection of flowers and not a weed to be seen. He would spend hours in his study and and "do not disturb" went without saying. We often went on camping holidays with the caravan and a small boat loaded up for the next exciting destination. He loved walking and I remember he managed to get us all lost, but in his words we were not lost. There were garden parties for his students so we had to be on our best behaviour. The garden photo was taken in the early 1980s.'

He was always there for every special occasion. A pair of his socks would be tied with green garden string for a stocking for Christmas. Christmas morning would be special; he would take us walking in Ashton

Court so we could come home to our Christmas dinner. A coal fire in the sitting room made you feel so warm and cosy as he would hand out the presents, one at a time. A ritual we now keep with our family. Oh, and there was always a big hug, if needed.'

John and Rosemary are pictured here in front of their home, Eastfield Lodge, c.1987 with two of their grandchildren James and Matthew, the younger one.

PART 3

OTHER OCCUPANTS AND THEIR HOMES

CARMARTHEN ROAD - 6

Micky Torpy reported that their long-time neighbour, Lorna Wells, of 6 Carmarthen Road had sadly passed away in December 2011. Mrs Wells was an extraordinary woman, still driving in her 90s, as bright as a button and a well-known Methodist in Henleaze and Westbury. The Wells family had lived at 6 Carmarthen Road, as long as, if not longer than the Torpy family at 8. Lorna was survived by her sons David and Allan and daughter Rosemary.

CARMARTHEN ROAD - 7

Micky Torpy brought to our attention the Rev. George Smith Winter who translated "Peep of the Day" into Cree (Indian) in 1898. He returned from Canada to Bristol with his family in 1899. They lived at 12 Fairfield Road - according to the 1901 and 1911 censuses, before moving to 7 Carmarthen Road - date unknown.

George had married Emma Elizabeth Ann Milton in 1879. Their daughters Dora and Josephine were born in 1889 and 1891 respectively in York Factory, Canada. Their three sons Percy, Walter and Alfred appear on censuses with birth years of 1886, 1893 and 1896.

George Smith Winter was a Church of England Clerk in Holy Orders. He was ordained as a deacon in 1879. He was ordained as a priest in 1880 in Moosoneee (Ontario, Canada) and worked for the Church Missionary Society at York Factory, Manitoba from 1879 - 94. He was then a missionary at Sturgeon Lake, Saskatchewan from 1894 - 1899.

George lived with his daughters, Dora and Josephine at 7 Carmarthen Road (also known as the College of St Barnabas) until he died in 1940 aged 86. His wife, Emma had died in 1933 aged 80. Former neighbour Micky believes that George may have been Chaplain to the Royal School for the Blind in Henleaze in his latter years. His two spinster daughters continued to live on the first floor of 7 for the remainder of their lives. The ground floor was rented out to trainee clergymen who were training in Bristol.

Grace Theodora Winter and Marjorie Josephine Winter, the daughters, were better known as Dora and Josephine respectively. They are recalled by several local residents, including Micky, who remembered that the ladies had been brought up with the Cree Indians in Canada. During the 1950s they showed him and his sister their buckskin clothes and snow shoes which they had used as children. They both spoke Cree. Dora and Josephine ran a group known as the King's Messengers at St Peter's Church, Henleaze, possibly up until they died in 1965 and 1969 respectively. It was apparently a junior missionary branch that operated on a national basis

Dora and Josephine had given Micky a sample of Cree Indian beadwork at that time which he treasured for many years. However, when he was downsizing in 2014 he decided to kindly pass on the sample to Veronica Bowerman for the Henleaze Book archives – see photo.

CARMARTHEN ROAD - CROFT COTTAGE

Michael Torpy recalled that next to his former home, 8 Carmarthen Road, was a detached house called Croft Cottage. In the 1950s it was occupied by an elderly spinster Mildred Baker, who was the sister of Lady White. She was visited by Lord and Lady White in their chauffeur-driven Bristol, which had curtains in the windows. Miss Baker's live-in maid was called Ada. Micky became great friends with Miss Baker and used to run errands to the Henleaze shops for her. Occasionally for a treat he was taken in the chauffeur driven car to Whiteladies Road when Miss Baker and Lady White went shopping. Sadly she died when he was eight or nine years old.

EASTFIELD

The first "gentleman's residences" in Eastfield were built in the 1820s on land known as Eastfield Six Acres belonging to Sir Henry Protheroe of Cote House, Westbury-on -Trym. As a result of the age of these buildings many of them – although by no means all - have been included as Grade II listed buildings by English Heritage. This area has the highest density of listed buildings in Henleaze.

We are still researching the listed properties in this area and welcome any information that readers might have.

EASTFIELD TERRACE

Limestone quarrying was a major activity in the Henleaze area. These terraced properties were built around the 1860s to accommodate quarrymen and their families locally.

Two stable buildings at the rear of nos. 11-15 were approached through a double door entrance above no 15.

Some of the houses have retained the original boot-scrapers built into the property by the front door

HENLEAZE GARDENS - 19

When Alfred Harrison established his rope and twine making business (Harrison and Co. (Bristol) Ltd) in 1907, he was living in Henleaze Gardens and, by 1911, had moved to 32 Downs Park East. Richard Griffiths, his great-grandson, suspects that Alfred may have sold or given 19 Henleaze Gardens to his daughter Olive and her husband Herbert Griffiths on their marriage in 1910. Herbert lived there until his death in 1946 and Olive until 1966 when she died.

Rear garden of 19 Henleaze Gardens believed to have been taken around 1910–1916.

Here is a photo of them taken of Herbert and Olive Griffiths on their first wedding anniversary in 1911 in Llandudno.

Richard Griffiths added:

'When Olive (my grandmother) was still alive, she had the first floor of 19 Henleaze Gardens, while (one her sisters), Margery had the rather attic-like second floor. (More details can be seen on Margery who embarked on a career as a writer under the name of Margaret Harrison.) Another sister Gladys, who was always called Chris, lived on the ground floor. Her second name was Christine. In my grandfather's photo albums there is a picture of a girl.

'I suspect that this is Christine; she would have been just about 17 when the picture was taken and Olive would have been 20.'

Three photos courtesy of Richard Griffiths.

WALLISCOTE AVENUE - 10

In 2015 an email pointing out a previous text error was received from Ian Thomas, now living in North Dorset:

I was fascinated to see on page 80 of The Henleaze Book a reference to 10 Walliscote Avenue, a house into which I moved as a one year old in 1939 and left for university in the mid-1950s. The text says it was owned by the Seal family but in fact my parents bought it from Audrey Seal's parents, Mr and Mrs Sydney Briginshaw. At that time I believe Audrey's future husband Eric still lived with his parents in Henleaze Park Drive. They were married in Henleaze very soon after World War Two.

This was a mistake which has been confirmed by Carole Gough, one of Audrey Seal's daughters. 10 Walliscote Avenue was the home of Mr and Mrs Sydney Briginshaw and their daughter Audrey until 1939 when they moved to the Crescent. Audrey married Eric Seal in 1945. Her story is included in the earlier part of this book.

'The figure of £750 was mentioned as the buying price in 1932 which is about the same as I believe my parents paid seven years later – no house inflation in the 1930s! My parents left the house in 1966 and went to Clevedon. They sold to a Mr and Mrs Whitehead.'

MANY MEMORIES FROM HARBURY ROAD

From time to time the Henleaze Book receives enquiries from people who are trying to tie up some loose threads in their family tree with possible Henleaze connections.

Coincidentally, several people have been in touch about Harbury Road, off Wellington Hill West, Henleaze in recent years.

Pete Northey was researching the lives of his late parents and grandparents.

He asked if anyone had any information on two Harbury Road properties.

The building, later the Coop, where Western Tool & Design was believed to have been located.

4 Harbury Road – where his grandfather, William Bailey, had an ironmongery shop. Pete Northey's mother's father, William Bailey, pictured here, died in 1957.

From around 1932-1950 William ran his own ironmongery shop, pictured here, at 4 Harbury Road. (Both photographs from the Northey collection.)

Pete's father, Basil George Richard Northey (known as Dick to his working colleagues) worked for Western Tool & Design in Harbury Road from 1942 – 1946. He was an engineering designer who afterwards moved to Thrissell's, later to become Masson-Scott-Thrissell of Easton.

Can anyone help with their memories of Basil Northey and Western Tool during the WWII years?

In later years Basil Northey became a permanent deacon at The Sacred Heart Catholic Church in Grange Court Road. Michael Corrigan remembers Basil well as a devout, caring and helpful parishioner, much involved in all parish activities. Stewart Craddy also remembers Basil as a Deacon, parishioner and a contributor to the parish magazine of which he was editor for some time. Basil died suddenly in 1987.

Another Henleaze Book contact was a former pupil of St Margaret's

School - Angela Sundquist (née Batt).

'I remember Harbury Road in the 50`s and 60`s very well, Mr Cohen the fishmonger, Miss Scudamore the wool shop, further down Fred Palmer and his mother the newsagents, and then Mr Batten the butchers. It was a real community. (The Batt family lived in an adjacent road then.) I was fifteen when my mother died very suddenly, and the kindness shown by these shopkeepers I doubt you would find today.'

Angela's paternal grandfather was Charles Batt, also known as Charlie (1890 – 1965).

He is shown here in this 1930s photograph from the Batt collection.

On 7 February 1941 he started Western Tools Designs Ltd with a drawing office in Harbury Road and a manufacturing unit of approximately five sheds and various other buildings, some of which were rented from a Mr Clark, a short distance away in Kelston Road, Southmead.

Charles appointed himself Chairman and his eldest son, Eric, Managing Director. Kenneth, his second son and father of Angela, was also in the business, but did not have a title.

The family employed around 110 people mainly producing taps and dies for threads for torpedoes etc. and production jigs and tools used by the Admiralty during World War II.

After that time they made electric fires and steel-framed furniture until the factory closed down. Charles spent a lot of capital researching the best way to make ceramic bars for electric fires.

On Friday, 5 March 1948 there was a fire which the Bristol Evening Post confirmed with their article headlined 'Fire at the Factory caused by Thieves?'

Eric Batt, the Managing Director at that time and eldest son of Charles, was interviewed by the newspaper for their article. It appears that there was a tool shed containing a large amount of inflammable paint which caused the fire to burn so fiercely.

Later in 1948, as a result of the fire and an increase in purchase tax on luxury goods to 33% and its adverse effect upon trading, the creditors resolved upon voluntary liquidation. Charles subsequently took various part-time jobs with local companies but decided to retire in the 1950s.

Angela remembers him as quite a remarkable man. 'At 25 he developed TB, and then had a lung removed. He suffered stomach ulcers and other problems, landing up having a large part of his stomach removed. He was quite a character, a good engineer although not a good businessman, but he had immense compassion. When he and my grandmother moved to Hallen Road, Henbury, as a teenager I would cycle over and he often would have an elderly tramp sat in the garden enjoying a cup of tea and piece of cake. He disliked people who were quick to judge. As a child I was a bit scared of him, but as I got older I admired his spirit. He died in 1965.'

One of the long term residents of Harbury Road, Mike Stephenson, a local history enthusiast, was able to supply a list of the businesses with even numbers in Harbury Road researched from Kelly's directories.

1956

2 - Ernest Bunker – grocer

4 - Mr Borne – ironmonger

6 - Edgar Thorn – butcher

8 - Charles Palmer – newsagent

10 - Miss J Scudamore – draper

12 - Newman Cohen – fish, fruit & vegetable

14 - Asco Ltd – scale makers.

1968

2 - Abbot & Palmer – consulting engineers

4 - Elite – bakers

6 - L Batten – butcher

8 – H Preston – dental technician

10 - Harbury News – newsagent

12 - Elite – fruit & vegetable

14 - Asco-Bizerba – scale makers.

The article published in 2016 in the Bristol Times about Harbury Road (off Wellington Hill West) and the history of its shops produced several emails, photos and telephone calls including the following memories, so many thanks to the people concerned, including Chris and Libby Bloor, C Dumbleton, Mike Stephenson, Mary Wilson (nee Powell), Patsy Reed (nee Parry), Mont Meredith and Derek Marchant.

In 2016 the Stephensons had a delightful chat over a cup of tea with Patsy Parry in their Harbury Road home.

Mike reported that it was strange to think that Patsy had been living just around the corner from them for a few years. The memories she shared were all as clear as crystal to her after 50-plus years! It was a pleasure to learn about her dad Gordon and the houses and shops he built in the 1930s.

Gordon sadly died at the quite young age of 54 while in retirement in Paignton, I say retired because he had a 50-room hotel there! Mike commented that it was a pleasure to meet Patsy.

Patsy Reed (nee Parry) has now returned to live in Henleaze.

1939 – Patsy's parents, Gordon and Ada (known as Pat) married at Cockington in Devon and were given stained glass windows as a wedding present for their home in Wellington Hill West. These were covered over during the war and did not see the daylight until 1946.

'Gordon Parry had an air raid shelter built in their garden for WWII and, because there were no fridges in those days, the grocer neighbours, the Bunkers, kept their butter stock there. Gordon also had a gate built in his back garden to enable the Bunkers to share the shelter.

'They used to share their eggs, fruit and vegetables with their neighbours. They were thrilled when one of their chickens managed to sit on 12 eggs at the same time and they all hatched out. Sadly they were all cockerels, so the neighbours were not too pleased with the noise early in the morning. However Gordon decided as Christmas approached to have the cockerels killed by the local butcher. They were then given as presents to various nearby residents.'

Patsy remembers the following shops from the early 1950s:

No.12. Newman and Cohen (who were Jews) – fishmongers and greengrocers.

After Mrs Cohen went blind, the family collected money for Guide Dogs for the Blind and received various trophies marking their efforts and generosity.

No.3. Mrs Edith Prim (a widow) ran the ice cream shop and sold Lyons ice cream at 2d each – (late 1940s/early 1950s price!) less than one penny, post decimalisation.

Patsy can remember the waste ground opposite their house being flooded on one occasion. She recalled Waterdale House on the other side of Wellington Hill West and its large boating lake. The former was demolished in the 1960s and the latter filled in to provide land for new housing in the 1960s – known as Waterdale Close and Gardens.

C. Dumbleton recalled the shops on the other side of Harbury Road in the 1940s and 1950s - the odd numbers.

'No.1 was a hairdresser's shop.

'No.3 (listed in the 1947 edition of Kelly's as Mrs Edith Prim, confectioner) was a cake shop / private library called I think "Mrs Prim's Pantry" and, more intriguing, the shop where the local housewives gathered to exchange all the local gossip, especially after the murder in Wellington Hill West! (Ann Cornock was charged with the murder of her husband, Cecil Cornock, following his suspicious death. She was acquitted in 1946.)

'Then there was a gap where three houses were subsequently built in the 1950s, before the Coop building. The Coop was originally three shops - a dairy which sold milk tokens and, again after the war, very watery ice creams and not much else! The middle shop was a grocery shop complete with a pulley system in the middle for the transport of the money (the same as in Morgan's on Gloucester Road – now replaced by Maplin Electronics) and lastly a butcher's shop.

'No.11. The Bristol Coop Society Ltd was expanded to include a butcher area in 1940.' (Only two departments, dairy and grocery, are listed at this location in the 1939 edition of Kelly's Directories.)

Patsy Reed (nee Parry) was able to supply this picture of Harbury Road at the time when the shops were first opening and the road was being built. One of the men standing in the centre is Gordon Parry.

Mary Wilson (nee Powell) recalls:

'I was born at No.6 Harbury Road (shown in the following photo) in July 1933 and we lived there until I was nearly five years old.

'This photo was taken in 1932, the year before I was born. The tall man in white on the left is my father, William Powell and the shorter man his brother, Uncle Ted, Mr E. D. Powell. The little boy is my brother, Richard, aged three years.

'Richard can remember quite a bit more, so between us we have recalled the following from the information on the shops previously mentioned.

'In 1938 Mr W.H.E Powell, our father, sold his shop at No 6 to a Mr. Bingham. Edgar Thorn is shown as the butcher here in the 1947 edition of Kelly's directory.

'At that time there was a lane leading to the back of the shops by No. 8 - Charles Palmer, the newsagent.

'Our aunt, Miss Mary Powell ran the drapery shop here from 1933 -

1935 at No. 10. We presume that she then sold the house to Mrs. Prim, the sister-in-law of the Prims at No.3 on the opposite side of the road who sold cakes, pastries and ice cream. Part of No.10 appears to have been rented then to the Misses Pask. One of these sisters was a vet. The ground floor of the building seems to have been run as a drapery shop by the Scudamores. (This property was shown in Kelly's in the name of Herbert Scudamore, draper in 1947, and Miss J Scudamore subsequently in 1956.)'

Mont Meredith wrote that he was an apprentice in 1959 and the young man standing in the Asco doorway.

'Mr and Mrs Ellison lived above the shop, Mr Ellison being the foreman for Asco. The company was taken over by Bizerba around 1965.'

Derek Marchant wrote:

'We read your article on Harbury Road with great interest having lived at No.5 for a period of three years, around 1975.

'At that time we used the Coop shop at No.11 (now the Henleaze Business Centre) which then had the remains of a dairy at its rear. From the 1990s the nearby Tesco's store (on Golden Hill) took most of the trade from this once very busy shopping area.

'Our rank of three adjacent houses (5, 7 and 9) was built in the 1950s. It is interesting to read of the building delay on our side of the road. We suffered a couple of times with overflowing sewerage problems under the house and on one occasion it was necessary for the Council to lime the area beneath it. We were told unofficially that they were 'Jerry built' houses as the drains had been laid level with no fall to an outlet.'

Derek also recalled one dark evening hearing the sound of breaking glass and spotted a man with a suitcase by the side door to Harbury News.

'We had no house telephone and the call box was located right outside of the shop so I ran all the way to another telephone box (pictured here) at the bottom of Wellington Hill to summon the Police. (Waterdale House can be clearly seen on the right behind the telephone box.)

'They duly arrived like a scene from The Sweeney, screeching brakes and four cars from different directions blocked the road and a surge of police tore into the shop.

'A burly policeman next arrived on our doorstep asking if I was the culprit who had rung 999. With a chuckle he told me that the individual was the shop owner who had forgotten his house keys after returning home late from a business trip and had decided to break into his own shop!

'Apologies next day but I was at least thanked for being so vigilant.'

In spite of massive local protest and subsequent appeals the development of Tesco's went ahead at nearby Golden Hill in 1993.

Mike Stephenson, a local resident, took and sent photos of the even numbered shop in 1996 to former local resident Patsy Parry to show how the road had changed since she left in 1950.

Patsy was the daughter of their builder and was then living in the Devon area. Many of the shops in Harbury Road providing food had closed down and had been replaced with service industries around the time Tesco's opened in 1993.

PART 4

SOME INTERESTING LARGER BUILDINGS AND THEIR OCCUPANTS

BURFIELD HOUSE, WESTBURY ROAD

Burfield House and its estate of fifteen acres on the main road from Clifton to Westbury-on-Trym were sold to Mr Symes on 14 June 1877 for £8,050. He lived there for many years and during that time he became Sheriff of Bristol in 1887 and was appointed a JP in 1889. He served a total of six times as Mayor and Lord Mayor (1893, 94, 95, 96, 1902 & 03) and became an Alderman in 1895. He was knighted at Osborne House in January 1898 and died in 1908 at the age of 71.

In 1905 a sub-committee of Red Maids' Governors had recommended a move from Denmark Street to larger premises. By the autumn of 1908 Burfield House, one of several houses being considered, was regarded as a suitable site. After extensive alterations, in 1911 the move took place during the summer holidays. The dedication of the school by the Bishop of Bristol took place on 16 October. The school fields were temporarily let to a farmer, so sheep and cattle grazed there.

The girls thought Burfield beautiful and were impressed by its rural surroundings. There were four dormitories instead of two and each girl had her own cubicle with a curtain that could be drawn across for privacy. The four bathrooms on each floor were particularly welcomed, after those in Denmark Street which were all in the basement.

In 1916, overwhelmed by the appalling stream of casualties from the Somme, the Red Cross asked for the use of the building as a hospital. Two hundred beds were proposed and the Red Cross agreed to meet all the costs of the School's temporary move to Manor Place, Clifton, plus re-instatement for the Westbury premises ate the end of the War. The girls were not able to return to Burfield until after the beginning of 1920 because of extensive and necessary repairs. In the 1930s a new classroom block was built in the grounds and further building added in the 1970s.

(Photo courtesy of Red Maids was taken during the early 1900s.) Burfield House operates as the administration centre for the school. In 2014, after extensive renovations, it was decided to highlight the heritage of this important historic building by reinstating its original name. So what had been previously known as the Main Building for many years was called Burfield House again.

KENTON MEWS - 7, HENLEAZE PARK FARM /THE BRIARS

This property was originally known as Henleaze Park Farm. It is shown on the first Ordnance Survey map of the area dated 1881.

The 1911 census also shows the property as Henleaze Park Farm and the occupants then as Samuel Bennett and his family. At this time Mr Bennett used to drive daily, by pony and trap, to his paper and stationery business in the city. In the 1980s John and Pat Spiller, owners of the property at that time, were given this photo of the house by Miss Bennett, the daughter (then living in Westbury Park). It was taken when her parents owned the property.

The architecture of this building is very similar to that of nearby Claremont House built in the 1850s - now a school for special needs. The Briars was approached by a narrow country lane until 1976 when it was replaced by a tarmac road named Kenton Mews with six new properties leading up to it as no.7, at the end of the cul de sac.

The mounting block still stands to the left of the entrance to the drive of the former Henleaze Park Farm. It would have been very useful for the Bennetts and previous owners. The wall on its left is part of the original boundary wall of the Henleaze Park estate.

WESTBURY ROAD - 125, THE HERMITAGE

These two photos are from the Michael Brooks' collection.

Following a telephone call and emails from Michael Stoate in 2013 we have now compiled the following information on the Hermitage.

This large secluded detached property at 125 Westbury Road is believed to have been built in the early 1800s – perhaps at the same time as nearby Burfield House.

1840 – Tithe Map - The property is shown as occupied in grounds marked 1027.

1850s - The house is thought to have been occupied by E Gwyer

1861 Census – shows James Michell as Head of Household, a mine proprietor, aged 66 with various visitors and three servants – a cook, a housemaid and a groom/gardener.

According to the Troopers Hill website, http://www.troopers-hill.co.uk/ James' business venture in Crews Hole failed in 1856 but he continued to be involved in mining in Cheshire while still living in Bristol.

The Bristol Gazette of 4 December, 1862 reported that 'a shocking accident occurred on Thursday morning last' to Mr Michell, of the Hermitage, Westbury-on-Trym, which terminated fatally. It is reported that his foot slipped as he turned round to talk to his agent while ascending the pit and he fell over 30 feet to the bottom.'

1871 Census - shows Rice Wasbrough as Head of Household, a Physician and Surgeon, aged 56, his wife Frances aged 59, a sister-in-law aged 52, one boarder, three servants – a cook, a parlour maid and a manservant.

1881 Census - shows Rice Wasbrough as Head of Household, aged 66 and his wife Frances aged 69. Here they have two female boarders and two servants – a cook and parlour maid.

1901 Census - shows John Lennard as Head of Household, aged 56 and a Boot Manufacturer and his wife Ellen aged 64, two daughters, a son and daughter in law, two servants – a cook and a parlour maid.

c.1927 – 1938 Leonard Stoate and his family lived here. The family milling business amalgamated with Spillers in 1933 but the family were still actively involved in operations. The business continues as Stoate &

Sons http://www.stoatesflour.co.uk/ with Michael Stoate, the fifth generation family miller, and now operates near Shaftesbury in Dorset.

SOUTHMEAD ROAD - SOUTHMEAD MANOR

This house is situated near the junction with Wellington Hill West. The original Manor House at this location in Southmead in the Parish of Westbury was first mentioned in 1319 in the Worcester Register of Bishop Cobham who granted to Henry, son of Ralph and Isabel Croke 'licence to hear divine service in their Chapel so long as the rights and customs of the Parish Church are not injured.'

Manor House, pictured here, has been a children's nursery since 1994 but has kept many of the interior traditional features

In 1926 when the grounds (9 acres) and the house were sold off in 3 lots, a now-listed Grade II Gazebo was included. This is in the grounds of the police station. It is completely landlocked but can be clearly seen from the back gardens of some of the private properties in Lake Road and also from Glenwood Road. The architectural details of the building indicate that it was built in the late 17th or early 18th century. It is one of the earliest examples of garden architecture in Bristol.

It is hoped that the future of the Gazebo will become secure once planning permission is agreed with the new owners – details to be announced at a later date. (The photo was taken by Julie Kaye, local resident.).

More about the previous owners of this historic property may be found in The Henleaze Book
https://sites.google.com/site/henleazebook/

PART 5

FORMER LODGES AND ESTATE WORKERS' HOMES

CLAREMONT LODGE

This property was originally the lodge cottage for the adjacent Claremont House, now a school for Special Needs. The lodge was renovated and extended in the 1980s and fronts Henleaze Park.

It had previously been the home of the chauffeur for Claremont House. In 1913 the adjacent garage was doubled in size and an inspection pit built in with a tin for collecting oil by the last private owners of Claremont House, the Bruce Coles. In the 1950s the chauffeur, who wore a black leather gaitered uniform, enjoyed driving Mrs Bruce Cole in large yellow Buick which was housed in the garage. He would often take her to Henleaze Road where the respective shop owners would come out to the car to discuss shopping needs. The property is shown on the 1880s ordnance survey map.

CLAREMONT COURT

The stables of Claremont House were situated at the top of Henleaze Park and were used a football changing quarters by the local primary schools before being renovated as housing in the 1990s and named Claremont Court.

The adjacent property within this new complex was the house of the gardener of Claremont House. The property is shown on the 1880s OS map.

HENLEY GROVE LODGE AT 84 HENLEAZE ROAD

84 Henleaze Road was the former main lodge for Henley Grove

Mansion as shown on the 1841 tithe map. It was still used as the main entrance to the mansion until Holmes Grove and Henley Grove were constructed. In 1898 R Byrne, who was responsible for the pasture land and farm buildings of the mansion lived there.

In the early 1900s it was occupied by the sister of Mrs Bruce Cole and her husband. (Mrs Bruce Cole was the last private owner of Claremont House.) The architecture is very similar to a lodge in St Anne's, Bristol.

HENLEY GROVE LODGE AT 132 HENLEAZE ROAD

132 Henleaze Road, the smaller former lodge for Henley Grove Mansion, was built in 1844 and is shown on the 1880s OS map. It is located by The Drive junction and is now known as Grove Lodge. It was the other smaller lodge for Henley Grove Mansion. It has very distinctive black and white timbering at the gable end facing on to Henleaze Road. According to the 1903 this Lodge only had a small footpath leading to the Mansion.

Tom Graveney, who played cricket for Gloucestershire and was one of England's finest batsmen, lived here for five years after marrying local girl Jackie Brookman in 1952.

SPRINGFIELD HOUSE LODGE AT 18 HENLEAZE ROAD

The former Springfield Lodge is located near the Downs Park East junction. Its present owners, Mr and Mrs Payne, found the date of 1727 in the building which would appear to confirm that it is the oldest inhabited building in Henleaze. It is a most attractive property as the photo shows, richly decorated in Tudoresque style with gabled windows of Tudor and Italian mix.

The property is shown on the 1840 Tithe map. The 1841 census shows that the occupants at that time were Thomas Badman, gardener,

30, Harrier Badman, wife, 30, Samuel, son, 6, William, son, 4 and Ann, daughter, 2.

The 1861 census shows the property as Springfield Lodge and the occupants James Graham, gardener and his family. The 1911 census shows the property as Northumberland Lodge and the occupants as John Britton, gardener and bailiff and his family. Unfortunately, the deeds of the present owners only date back to the 1930s when the Springfield/Northumberland House estate was broken up and sold. The lodge then became a private property on 4 October 1937.

The photo of the lodge was taken in 2014 by the author.

RUSSELL GROVE - 31 AND 33 - SPRINGFIELD COTTAGES

These are now known as 31 and 33 Russell Grove and are shown on the 1840s tithe map. They are believed to be part of the Springfield Estate. This seems to be confirmed by the 1900s OS map which clearly shows that the only footpath to and from these cottages led to

Springfield House (later Northumberland House School for Girls). The 1871 Census shows the occupants as John Clark aged 48, an agricultural labourer, Lydia Clark, his wife aged 49 as a cook in domestic service, their sons William aged 13 as an errand boy to a grocer, and John aged 9 as a scholar. The 1881 Census shows that John and Lydia are still there but their occupations have changed – John to a gardener in domestic service and Lydia to a lodging housekeeper. Other occupants in the property then were Joseph Davis aged 26 who was a footman and Harriett Hort aged 21 who was a servant.

PART 6

NON-RESIDENT CONNECTION (1885) HUGH CONWAY - ACCOUNTANT & BEST-SELLING AUTHOR

Frederick John Fargus (1847 - 1885), the eldest son of an auctioneer, was born in Bristol in 1847. The 1851 census shows the family living at Kingsdown Parade. The 1861 census shows Frederic Fargus, his father, as a widower, living in Somerset Street with three young sons. Frederick was then aged 14. It was intended that Frederick should join his father's business, but in 1860, at the age of thirteen, he decided to enlist with the training-ship "Conway" in the Mersey. In deference to his father's wishes, however, he gave up the idea of becoming a sailor, and returned to Bristol where he was articled to a firm of accountants. On his father's death in 1868 he took over the family business. The 1871 census shows Frederick as head of the family with his two younger brothers living in Vale House, Westbury-on- Trym. Frederick, as a clerk, had written the words for various songs, adopting the nom-de-plume Hugh Conway in memory of his days on the training-ship.

Mr. Arrowsmith, the Bristol printer and publisher, took an interest in his work, and Fargus's first short story appeared in *Arrowsmith's Miscellany*. In 1883 Fargus published through Arrowsmith his first long story, *Called Back,* of which over 350,000 copies were sold within four years. On medical advice Frederick John Fargus (aka High Conway) travelled to the Mediterranean where he died of typhoid fever in Monte Carlo in 1885. He was buried in Nice. *A Family Affair,* published posthumously in 1885, was loosely based on Henleaze (Oakbury) and Bristol (Blacktown). It is about two brothers named Talbert who lived at Hazelwood House (based on Francis and Charles Savage who lived at Springfield House until their deaths in the 1890s.) Later this property became Northumberland House School for Girls.

PART 7

HISTORY OF ST GOAR SCHOOL

Following on from Brian Robbins' memories and the archives of the Bristol Record Office, we are now able to provide some interesting information on St Goar School for Boys which was in existence for 76 years (1888 – 1964).

From time to time something completely forgotten in the passage of time is highlighted and the search begins to find more information. St Goar School, Bristol, attended by Brian Robbins in the 1930s, was one of these examples. Brian also found several old photos of his time at the school which was considered then to be a first class prep school preparing the boys for Clifton College.

Since reading through the information of the history of the school researched from the Bristol Record Office, Brian was able to add the following:

'Many thanks for forwarding all the information you have garnered, it was very interesting. Regarding the name St Goar - as it so happens my wife Jill and I went on a driving/camping holiday in 1955, the year after we were married, and drove through St. Goar, but I had no idea then of its connection with my old prep school.

'The bit on health reminded me that we walked to school one Monday morning and met excited boys coming back who told us we would be sent home as we were all in quarantine as a boy called Tipper had scarlet fever. We were not supposed to mix, but I remember clearly it was fine weather and we spent the week or fortnight (I can't remember which) mucking about on the Northumberland Avenue estate which was being built at that time.

'I think we had a school tie and a school cap with I think two circular red and white rings. (Editor's note: It may be a coincidence, but the colours of the town of St Goar are red and white.) Other than that no further gems of information come to mind.

'I think in my time Mr Elsworthy took gym on Saturday mornings in Westbury Village Hall at the top of a steep hill out of Westbury-on-Trym. I recall Miss Wakefield who took Cubs and another teacher called Miss Bolton who had a long neck!'

With many thanks to Brian and also to the Bristol Record Office, we are able to give more details of this school. Hopefully this information will generate memories from other former pupils?

St Goar School was founded in 1888 and was so named after the Patron Saint of the Rhineland town of St Goar. Three sisters, the Misses Agnes, Alice and Florence Lemon (who would have then been aged 35, 33, and 31) had previously spent a holiday on the Rhine and were charmed by the then Rhineland village, St Goar hence the school's name.

In its early days the School, like many others, was situated in Clifton. After WWI it moved to various locations in Henleaze, Westbury-on-Trym and Westbury Park and remained in that area until the early 1950s before finding its final location at Julian Road, Sneyd Park. In 1952, the long-looked-for opportunity of a more suitable building arrived, and the building in Sneyd Park was purchased. This gave the school a house much better fitted for a school, and able to hold the increased numbers in comfort; there was also a large playground.

St Goar School (1888-1964) celebrated its 75th anniversary with a dinner on Friday, 22 March, 1963 at the Grand Spa, Clifton.

Sadly the school, over time, became financially unviable and was only able to continue until 1964. The parents were all notified by letter offering several solutions including a merger with nearby Braidlea

Preparatory School. At that time there were also a few boarding places available at Walton Lodge School where the Head, Mr Newman, was taking up the position of Assistant Headmaster.

ITS DIFFERENT LOCATIONS

During its 76 year existence the school moved on no less than six occasions:

1888 - 5 Alma Road, Clifton

1906 (May) - 75 Pembroke Road, Clifton

1923 (September) - 72 Downs Park East

1926 (September) - 2 The Grange

c1929 - 131 Westbury Road

1946 - Alveston Lodge, Westbury Park (This property was subsequently acquired by Muller's Orphanage in the early 1950s and was intended to house older boys and girls in advanced education in the city. It is currently owned by St Christopher's School.)

1949 - Julian Road, Sneyd Park until its closure in 1964.

HEADS

1888 – Three sisters – the Misses Agnes, Alice and Florence Lemon.

1898 (May) – 1928. Miss Helen Peake, who died in 1939, is shown as Joint Head with Miss Rose in the 1929 Kelly's directory.

Miss Rose (1929-1946)

Rev Paul Harper (1946-1947)

Mr David Newman (1947–1964)

In 1888 the school appears to have been set up and initially run by three sisters, Misses, Agnes, Alice and Florence Lemon at Alma Road, Clifton

In 1898 it was taken over by Miss Helen Peake at a new location - 75 Pembroke Road, Clifton. It continued there as a Prep school, chiefly for Clifton College.

It appears that Miss Peake remained Head when the school moved on to the Downs Park East and the Grange locations.

Miss Rose joined the Staff in 1925 and later became joint Head at 131 Westbury Road. On Miss Peake's death in 1939, became the sole Head. She continued as a teacher after Rev Paul Harper became Head in 1946. She retired in July 1959.

Rev. Paul Harper (1946 – 47) was Head at Alveston Lodge, Westbury Park

David Newman was the last Head 1947 – 1964 at Alveston Lodge, Westbury Park and Julian Road, Sneyd Park. He took an appointment as Assistant Head at Walton Lodge School, Clevedon, after the closure of St Goar.

SCHOOL FEES - 1900s - PEMBROKE ROAD

Per term, over 9s: 6 guineas (£6.30)

Under 9s: 5 guineas (£5.25)

Morning class for very young boys: 4 guineas (£4.20)

Dinner: 3½ guineas (£3.67)

Tea and Evening Preparation Class: 2 guineas (£2.10)

BOARDERS

Weekly 20 guineas: (£21.00) Full boarders: 25 guineas (£26.25)

1930s - The boys from St Goar enjoying their swimming lesson. Brian Robbins is on the extreme left. They used to go swimming twice a week in the indoor 'ladies' bath attached to the outdoor pool which is now Clifton Lido.

1937/8 - Pupils from St Goar. The photo was taken in the front garden of their school at 131 Westbury Road. Miss Rose, the head, is in the back row, far left. Brian Robbins is in the front row, sixth from the left.

July, 1939 - Sports' Day for the boys of St Goar in Canford Park, where an air raid shelter is being built. Brian Robbins is in the back row, right hand side, not looking at the camera.

FROM THE SCHOOL PROSPECTUS – 1950s – EDUCATION

Boys are taken between the ages of 5 and 14 years and are prepared for the English Public Schools' examinations. The school curriculum is based on the syllabus set out by "The Headmasters' Conference" and includes the following subjects: - Scripture, Arithmetic, Algebra, Geometry, English subjects, Latin, French, History, Geography and General Science. These subjects are taught in small forms, the average being 15 boys, by competent and qualified staff. The Junior School is taught basically by Froebel methods, whilst in the Senior School the emphasis is placed on the Three R's within the framework of the Common Entrance Exam Syllabus. Boys who show the necessary ability are prepared for Scholarships.

Time is also set aside each week for Drawing and Painting, Nature Study and Musical Appreciation. The younger boys do Handwork, Class

Singing and Percussion Band.

We demand of a boy his best efforts, and in return we give him that personal help and attention that is only possible in forms with small numbers, and we make his work as interesting as possible. Every effort is made to build up the characters and individuality of the boys and to instil in them the virtue of good manners.

SCHOOL HOURS - School opens with prayers at 9 o'clock each morning, and afternoon school ends for the lower forms at 3.15. The top forms stay on till 4.30 for Prep.

DISCIPLINE- This is under the direct supervision of the Headmaster. It is believed that boys appreciate good discipline, which is therefore firm, but not repressive. Rules are kept to the minimum, and every effort is made to ensure that the boys understand the reasons for them and that they must be obeyed.

Brian Robbins recalled that the school, in the 1930s, was divided into three houses -Westbury, Henleaze and Stoke. The teams from these Houses would compete in all aspects of sport and also in their work. Each House has a Captain who runs his House under the supervision of his Housemaster.

PARENTS' MEETING - A Parents' meeting is held once a term when the Headmaster can put any points to parents in general and can get their views. This has been found to be very useful and fosters a spirit of cooperation between the school and the parents. In addition it gives parents an opportunity of meeting the Staff.

GAMES- The proximity of the School to the Downs enables us to use reserved pitches on the Downs for most sports. Some games are also played at Canford Park.

In the summer the School plays cricket and, of course, several matches are played against schools in the neighbourhood. The School Sports are also held during this term with the exception of the Cross Country race which is run during the Easter term.

During the winter terms Association Football and hockey are played. All boys do Physical Training unless medically exempted, and instruction is given in boxing.

During the Christmas and Summer Terms most of the boys go with the School to Shirehampton Baths under the supervision of the school staff. Instruction is given to learners in the Small Bath, and more advanced coaching to those who can swim.

SITUATION- The school is situated a few minutes from the Downs and is serviced by the Nos. 2 and 22 bus routes.

HEALTH- The school has always maintained a particularly high standard of health and in order to maintain this at a high level, parents are asked to take every care that their children are not sent to school after they have been in contact with any infectious disease until the infection period has passed.

INSURANCE- The school belongs to an insurance scheme whereby parents are able, if they so wish, to insure themselves against school fees in cases of absence due to ill health. It can readily be understood that the school is unable to make reduction in fees to cover such absence.

FEES- The fees are inclusive; with the exception of a charge for printed books and handwork materials there are no necessary extras, those specified below are entirely optional.

Term Fees: -

For boys over 8 years = £28. 0. 0d (£28.00)

For boys under 8 years = £18. 0. 0d. (£18.00)

Dinners = £5.10. 0d (£5.50)

Sports fee = £1. 5. 0d (£1.25)

Extras: -

Music (Piano) = £2. 12. 6d. (£2.62)

Elocution = £2. 12. 6d. (£2.62)

Entry to Swimming Baths and transport = £1. 1. 0d. (£1.05)

All fees are payable in advance and a term's notice in writing is required before a boy leaves.

A reduction is allowed for younger brothers at the school, and special terms are available for the sons of Ministers and Clergy.

LIST OF CLOTHES

Grey shorts (corduroys are recommended), School Blazer

Grey Shirt (Winter Terms), White Shirt (Summer Terms)

School Tie, Belt, Pullover, Stockings, Brown Sandals (for indoor wear)

Long Trousers may be worn by boys in 2nd and 3rd forms

School Cap, Blue Raincoat

Black Shoes, Blue Football Shorts

House Football Jersey, School Football Stockings

White Sweater, Football Boots

White PT Shoes

Bag to hang on peg to hold games clothes

For Cricket: Cricket boots or shoes

School Outfitter: Messrs. Steer & Geary, The Mall, Clifton.

RULES:

DRESS– All boys will be properly dressed at all times. Caps will be worn on all occasions when out of the school grounds. Boys who throw or kick about any item of clothing will be punished.

MANNERS – All boys are expected to behave like gentlemen, caps will be raised to members of the staff, and to parents and their friends. The reputation of the school is largely judged by the behaviour of the boys outside the school. This in particular applies to boys on buses. They will remain in their seats, unless others are standing, and talk quietly.

GENERAL - There will be no talking after the second bell before prayers. At the first bell after breaks, boys will change their shoes, go to their classrooms and be in their desks by second bell.

After morning school, boys will wash their hands and line up quietly in the hall by Houses.

Boys will stand when a member of the staff or a visitor enters a classroom. There will be no running or pushing inside the school.

The back yard is OUT OF BOUNDS except when visiting the toilets or the cycle shed. Outdoor shoes will be worn at all times out of doors.
There will be no ragging or swinging on pegs in the changing room.
Bicycles must not be ridden in the school grounds. Boys may only visit the Tuck Shop after 4.15pm. Milk will be drunk at the beginning of break only. Selling or swapping are only permitted for stamp or similar collections. If in doubt about the value of an article, ask a member of staff.

Boys will endeavour to keep the school premises clean and tidy. Desks will be kept tidy, and all books treated with care and respect. Football boots will not be worn in the changing room.

OPEN SCHOOL DAYS - 1960s - Formal invitation cards were located in Bristol Record Office for the following dates:

Friday, 16 June 1961, Friday, 22 June, 1962 , Saturday, 15 June 1963

These Open Days were free and contained similar programmes:

10-noon: the building and staff were open to visitors.

From 2pm: Schools displays of PT, Boxing and Judo.

Miscellaneous stalls organised by the 'Friends of St Goar'.

St Goar School (Courtesy of the Bristol Record Office Ref 36773/5). This was the school's final location at Julian Road, Sneyd Park, Bristol, until July 1964.

75th ANNIVERSARY (1888-1963) - A dinner on Friday, 22 March, 1963 at the Grand Spa, Clifton marked the 75th anniversary of St Goar School. It was a formal, dinner jacket occasion with tickets costing 25/- (£1.25) per head.

The Programme for the evening included:

Loyal Toast - Mr W J Britton - Chairman, the Friends of St Goar School

THE SCHOOL - Proposer - Rt Hon R H Turton MC MP: Responder - Mr D Newman, Headmaster, The Friends of St Goar School Association

Proposer - Mr Martin McLaren, MP: Responder - Mr S C Shapcott

THE GUESTS – Proposer - D H Fox: Responder - Mr Martin Hardcastle MA (Acting Headmaster Clifton College)

A three course dinner was served with various wines – Red Burgundy, Beaujolais, White Bordeaux, Graves and Rose d'Anjou costing an additional 3/- (15p) per glass.

1964 – 8 FEBRUARY – LETTER OF SCHOOL CLOSURE

This was sent to all parents stating that due to continuing falling numbers it was no longer possible to run the school on an economic basis. The Head, David Newman, had been able to arrange with Mr Buckland, the Headmaster of nearby Braidlea School, for an amalgamation of the two schools in September, thus preserving an element of continuity for St Goar and most of its present pupils. Miss Nockolda, one of the teachers, was also moving to Braidlea in September. Mr Newman anticipated that the majority of the boys would also move to Braidlea as they prepared for the same examinations and had the same aims and outlook as St Goar. This should also ensure that the transition could be a smooth one for the boys.

Mr Newman wanted minimum disruption for the staff and boys, who would obviously be the most affected by the closure decision. A Parents' meeting was arranged for Friday, 14 February at which Mr Buckland,

Head of Braidlea, was present. Mr Newman explained the situation in greater detail. He also offered to discuss any individual problems with parents and to give any advice or help.

Mr Newman advised that he would be going to Walton Lodge School at Clevedon as Assistant Headmaster where there would be a few vacancies for boarders in September. He regretted having to make this decision and thanked parents on behalf of himself and his wife for all their help and support. It is believed that the school closed its doors in Julian Road, Sneyd Park, at the end of the school year in July 1964.

1964 - FINAL SCHOOL SPORTS DAY

Races included: Egg & Spoon, Slow Bicycle, Obstacle Race, Mother and Son, 80yards, 100yards, 220yards and 440 yards.

This must have been a bitter-sweet occasion for boys, staff and parents. Sadly we have not been able to locate any photos recording any of the events that took place on that day. Do you know of anyone that can help?

(Editor's note: The school crest is almost the same as the coat of arms for the town of Sankt/St Goar – see Wikipedia https://en.wikipedia.org/wiki/Sankt_Goar)

PART 8

ADDITIONAL INFORMATION

The cover was designed by the author, Veronica Bowerman. The front cover photo was taken by her on an Open Day at Henleaze Lake.in 2016. The back cover photo depicting a Dutch scene in a local stained glass window is courtesy of resident, Libby Bloor.

If you want to know more about Henleaze there are several other titles that can be found in the Henleaze Heritage range of books via this link. Feedback on the Amazon website about any of these publications would also be appreciated.

http://www.amazon.co.uk/Veronica-Bowerman/e/B001JS6O7U/

We do hope that you have found this book on some of the people that have lived in Henleaze interesting and informative? There may be someone that you feel should have been included? Please let us know via email henleazeheritage@gmail.com

It is often difficult to recall events from many years ago so should any of the information be inaccurate or needs clarification please let us know.

Feedback would also be appreciated on St Goar School, other schools and local history in the Henleaze vicinity.

Finally, if you have any photos of other information that could be of interest for future editions relating to local history in Henleaze please make contact with us.

ABOUT THE AUTHOR

Veronica Bowerman lived in Henleaze, a suburb of North West Bristol in England for nearly 40 years. They moved three times as the family grew - all within Henleaze!

However on retirement Veronica and her husband decided to move to the countryside and are now settled in the historic village of Wick St Lawrence, near Weston super Mare.

In the early 1970s, The Henleaze Society was formed. A newsletter was created and the Society was keen to have articles of local interest. Veronica volunteered to knock on doors of interesting historical properties in the area and interview the occupants. Residents were enthusiastic and often very generous with their time. One lady asked Veronica if she was from "Country Life"! Veronica had to disappoint her, but it didn't stop the interview, fortunately.

Veronica is a member of the Facebook team and a listed speaker for ALHA - Avon Local History and Archaeology – an umbrella organisation for more than 90 local history and archaeology societies in the South West.

Over the years, many residents had posed the question: "When are you going to produce a local history book on Henleaze?" With the help of her good friends, Sylvia Kelly, Ron Lyne and Elizabeth Herring the first edition of The Henleaze Book was produced in the 1990s and then, with the help of Redcliffe Press, the second edition was published in 2006.

PUBLICATIONS

HENLEAZE CONNECTIONS is the third paperback edition to be published. Previously published:

THE HENLEAZE BOOK - available through Amazon
http://www.amazon.co.uk/Henleaze-Book-Veronica-Bowerman/dp/0955356709

Amazon Customer - July 2015
'Arrived the next day thank you, also brilliant book.'

ST MARGARET'S: MEMORIES, MUSINGS & MERRIMENT
(now sold out and only available as an e-book)

E-BOOKS

From 2014, Veronica has published several e-books through KDP Amazon including:

1 - Henleaze Junior School - The Early Years
Feedback from Saff via Amazon - April 2015
'Henleaze was my home until 1972....how I miss it.
I attended 1955 until 1959. Some of the teachers' names I recognise, although I had thought that our dear Mr Charles went to Nigeria before reading this. Thank you Veronica et al.'

2 - Around the World in 80 Years - Retirement can be Fun!

3 - St Margaret's: Memories, Musings & Merriment
Feedback from Julie in March 2015 via Amazon
'Full of interesting facts and glad the history of this school is not lost forever. Fantastic.'
4 - Short Breaks. We All Need Them: Value for Money Ideas.
Published - January 2016

HERITAGE TRAILS

A free leaflet entitled The Henleaze Heritage Trails was published in 2013, thanks to funding via The Henleaze Society from the Neighbourhood Partnership. It has generated additional interest in the Henleaze area, particularly from local residents and various Bristol walking groups.

In 2015 a further leaflet with funding obtained from the Neighbourhood Partnership was created for the nearby suburb of Westbury on Trym, Bristol. Pdf copies can be obtained of these trails from this website: https://sites.google.com/site/henleazebook

LINKS TO PUBLICATIONS

For further details on these publications etc. please see The Henleaze Book website http://sites.google.com/site/henleazebook/   and also https://www.amazon.co.uk/Veronica-Bowerman/e/B001JS6O7U

Printed in Great Britain
by Amazon